MAKING YOUR PAPER

MARIANNE SADDINGTON

Photographs by Juan Espi
Illustrations by Marianne Saddington

NEW HOLLAND

First published in the United Kingdom in 1991 by
New Holland (Publishers) Ltd
37 Connaught Street, London W2 2AZ

ISBN 1 85368 140 7

House editors: Annlerie van Rooyen,
Jan Schaafsma
Designer: Janice Evans
Cover designer: Abdul Amien
Photographic stylist: Elaine Levitte
Indexer: Linda de Villiers

Typeset by Diatype Setting cc
Reproduction by Hirt & Carter (Pty) Ltd
Printed and bound in Singapore by Kyodo Printing
Co (Singapore) Pte Ltd

Endpapers: Japanese marbling on cotton paper.

Title page: Paper-cast of an African mask, woodcut
(by Thelma Harwood) and paper-cast of clay mould.

Contents

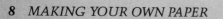

Introduction

As a calligrapher, I was initially attracted to paper-making in order to make, and write on, interesting and unusual paper. Once introduced to the technique, I was amazed at its simplicity. This led to a deep involvement in its history and a love of its variety and textural richness. The beauty of handmade paper is that no two sheets are alike.

With such a range of commercial papers available today, what is the attraction of making one's own? Many people enjoy handmade things. The unique texture and individual quality of handmade paper turns it into more than just a surface to write or draw on – it is an object of beauty in its own right.

Recycling wastepaper is a useful and relatively cheap way to reduce waste in our 'throw-away' society. Hunting for the raw materials used to make paper, or growing them in your garden, can also be exciting.

Paper-making need not be expensive, unless you want to make cotton paper or experiment with Japanese methods. All you need is a flat surface, access to water, an electric blender, absorbent fabric, a few hand tools and raw materials from your kitchen or garden.

Paper is such a commonplace thing, yet few people are familiar with paper-making techniques. These techniques are in fact very simple, allowing the amateur to make unusual and individual papers in a relatively short time. This book provides basic information about the processes involved in making paper, and gives simplified versions of both traditional and modern methods. It starts off with simple methods of recycling used paper, and progresses to making paper from various cultivated plants. Projects at the end of each chapter will increase your expertise and confidence, and spur you on to experiments of your own. There are also ideas for turning paper into creative gifts for family and friends, and for exploring the possibilities of paper art.

From left to right: vellum, Egyptian papyrus, beaten hibiscus bark, bark paper from Uganda and Japanese paper.

Chapter 1
What is paper?

'To be classed as true paper the thin sheets must be made from fibre that has been macerated until each individual filament is a separate unit; the fibres intermixed with water, and by the use of a sieve-like screen, the fibres lifted from the water in the form of a thin stratum, the water draining through the small openings of the screen, leaving a sheet of matted fibre upon the screen's surface. This thin layer of intertwined fibre is paper.'

DARD HUNTER, 1978

Essentially paper consists of the bonded fibres of plant material such as wood, straw, flax, hemp or cotton which is shredded, broken down to expose the cellulose in the fibres, then beaten to a pulp and mixed with water. If this mixture is drained through a sieve, the layer of fibrous material remaining on the sieve will dry to form paper. While making spinach soup, for example, you could produce a coarse sheet of spinach paper. If, after boiling and blending the spinach, you pour the pulpy mixture through a sieve, the thin, 'smoother' pulp will drain away (to be used for the soup), while the coarser material will remain in the sieve, forming a thin layer of matted fibres on the mesh. This layer of plant matter will dry into paper.

Paper as we know it today originated in China about two thousand years ago. Its invention is usually attributed to a Chinese eunuch, Ts'ai Lun, in 105 AD, although earlier examples have been recorded. Previously, Chinese scribes wrote on strips of wood or bamboo with a pointed stylus, but this was cumbersome and the strips of wood or bamboo were succeeded by books and scrolls of woven cloth. Ts'ai Lun took the idea a step further and began making paper from the bark of trees, hemp waste, old rags, fishnets and other plant fibres.

Since then many other plants have been used to make paper, including mulberry bark, hemp, China grass, bamboo and gampi. When paper was finally introduced to Europe a thousand years later, many of these plants were unavailable there, and most European paper was initially made from linen and cotton rags. The development of the printing trade increased the need for larger quantities of paper and at the beginning of the 19th century there was a search for a more economical and plentiful raw material. This discovery led to the use of refined wood pulp to make paper.

Wasp's nest and dried wood pulp.

The use of wood in paper-making was not new. It was first suggested to a French naturalist, de Réaumur, by his observations of the age-old nest-building activities of the wasp. The wasp rasps dry wood and chews it into a workable paste with which it makes a papery nest that is tough and highly water-resistant. This discovery later led chemists to experiment with the properties of wood as a substance for making paper.

The bulk of our paper today is made from chemically and mechanically refined wood pulp sprayed onto fast-moving belts of felt. Essentially the preparation and techniques are the same as for handmade paper, which was almost totally replaced by mass-production methods some 200 years ago.

In general artists still prefer handmade paper because of its strength and long-lasting qualities. In the West these properties are principally the result of a high cotton content. Cotton fibres are long, strong and resistant to the long-term destructive effects of light and atmosphere. The higher the percentage of cotton (and the lower the percentage of wood pulp) in the paper, the higher its quality. In the East the slow, gentle processing of long-fibred plants creates thin papers of remarkable tensile strength and durability.

What cannot be classed as paper?

Several substances we loosely classify as 'paper' cannot be regarded as true paper at all, for example papyrus, rice paper, parchment, vellum and the traditional bark papers of Central America and Polynesia.

Papyrus is a laminated material and not true paper, and was made from the plant *Cyperus papyrus* which grew abundantly on the banks of the Nile. Papyrus was prepared by slicing longitudinal strips from the inner stems of these plants, arranging them side by side in two or three layers, crosswise and lengthwise, soaking them in water and pressing them into a smooth surface.

Rice paper is a misnomer on two counts – it is neither made of rice, nor is it true paper. It is made from a tree, *Tetrapanex papyriferum* (formerly *Fatsia papyrifera*), which grows in the hills of northern Taiwan. Using a sharp knife, the 'paper' is cut spirally from the inner pith of the plant's stem.

Parchment and vellum as writing surfaces date back to at least 1500 B.C. and are still used today for diplomas and special

Making papyrus

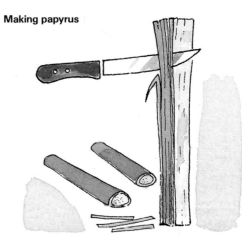

Slicing the outer green skin off the stem.

Layers of thin slices of pith are placed on top of each other at right angles.

Beating the layers gently with a mallet to facilitate bonding of the fibres.

manuscripts. Although they feel and look like paper, they are made from the stretched and treated skins of sheep and calves. Parchment is made from the fleshy side of the split skin of a sheep (strong leather is obtained from the wool side), while vellum is made from the whole skin of still-born or newly born calves or lambs.

The original inhabitants of Mexico, Central America and Polynesia used the beaten inner bark of the hemp plant and fig and mulberry branches to made a type of paper called huun, amatl and tapa.

Chapter 2
How to begin

The simplest way to make paper is to recycle wastepaper, for example computer paper or notepaper, by blending it with water to form a pulp. Having made enough pulp to form a few sheets of paper, a frame is placed on top of a piece of thick cloth, usually dressmakers' felt or old woollen blankets, and the pulp poured over the felt within the frame. The water is then removed by allowing it to drain and by placing a dry piece of felt on top of the wet paper to absorb excess water. A rolling pin can be used to remove even more water by rolling it firmly over the top piece of felt. The felt with its wet paper can then be hung up to dry. This chapter also includes information on how to store leftover pulp. To get started, make your first few sheets of paper by reading the instructions and carrying out the first two projects.

Basic equipment needed to make paper using the pouring method. *Clockwise from top right:* large plastic bottle, frames, embroidery frame, sponge, wooden spoon, jug, rolling pin, funnel, colander with netting and bucket.

Basic equipment for the pouring method

Frame (small picture or embroidery frame, chopsticks, strips of wood or piece of cardboard bent into a rectangular frame) in which to pour the paper pulp. The size should be approximately that of an A5 sheet of paper (210 x 148 mm).

Absorbent sponge for mopping water

Jug or large yoghurt carton for pouring pulp

Wooden spoon for stirring pulp

Rolling pin or smooth glass bottle (a wine bottle, for example) for pressing the wet paper sheets to remove excess water

Plastic bucket for storing pulp

Large plastic bottle for storing pulp

Funnel for draining leftover pulp

Electric blender for beating (or macerating) plant fibres into the pulp that will form paper. Traditionally the Japanese pounded their plants by hand with wooden mallets. For the purposes of this book, a kitchen blender with a capacity of about 1 ℓ is an adequate substitute.

Felt on which to pour the pulp to form sheets of paper. Traditionally felted woollen cloth was used, but dressmakers' felt works well and is easily obtainable at fabric centres. Use only the thinner natural fibre felt, not the thicker polyester variety. Old woollen blankets, cotton sheeting or thick calico can also be used, but avoid thin fabrics – the 'felt' must have a certain stiffness. (However, for the project at the end of this chapter you will be using cotton fabric instead of felt, as you will be ironing the paper dry.)

Net curtaining and colander to drain leftover pulp. Such pulp can be stored in sealed buckets or bottles as is, or drained through a sieve or colander lined with mesh to reduce the bulk and facilitate storing (*see* p 19 for further details). You can also use a cut-off nylon stocking for this purpose, or make a useful net drainage bag that fits a standard size bucket.

How to make a drainage bag

Cut a piece of net curtaining of 860 x 700 mm. Machine stitch the two shorter sides together, creating a tube, and then sew the bottom of the bag in the same way. Turn down 40 mm at the top of the bag, fold under the raw edge and machine stitch.

Net bag to fit a standard-sized bucket.

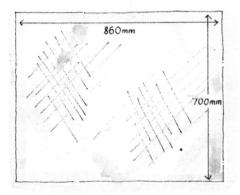

Net curtaining.

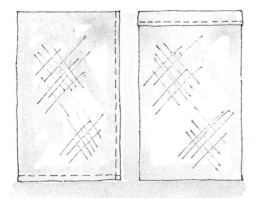

Sew sides and bottom seams.

Turn down top and hem.

How to make pulp

Recycled paper pulp can be made from tissues, computer paper, photocopying paper, wrapping-paper, brown paper, artists' watercolour paper, pastel paper, notepaper or envelopes, used on their own or in combination. Do not use heavily printed paper if you want to make long-lasting paper (*see* box below), and cut out and discard those parts of the paper with adhesive tape, glue, plastic or staples.

> **Note:** *Newspapers and magazines can be recycled, but must be boiled in detergent to remove the ink. Tear the paper into strips and boil it for about an hour in a solution of one tablespoon of washing-up liquid to 2 ℓ of water. Remove the scum that rises to the surface while boiling – this is the ink being lifted off the paper. After boiling, rinse the paper well before blending it to make pulp. There are some disadvantages to recycling newspapers – the paper is prone to acid attack, deteriorates rapidly and becomes brittle and yellow with age because of the impurities left in the original pulp by the processing method. It can be interesting to recycle newspapers as an experiment, but never use it to make long-lasting paper.*

First tear the paper into pieces measuring approximately 20 mm square and soak in water overnight. The better the quality of the paper, the smaller you need to tear the pieces and the longer they must be soaked. For example, tissues can be torn into quite large pieces and soaked for only 30 minutes, while Fabriano watercolour paper needs to be torn into pieces less than 20 mm square, and soaked for two to three days. You can speed up the process by pouring boiling water over the torn paper and allowing it to stand. Most paper will then be ready to macerate after an hour or two.

Once the paper has been soaked, it is macerated in an electric blender or food processor. Place a small handful of wet, torn paper and two cups of water in a blender, and blend for 15-30 seconds. Thick card or quality papers will take longer. After a while, experience will tell you how long to blend different kinds of paper. It is best to blend the paper for the *shortest possible time* – just long enough for the fibres to separate. Stop the machine after 15 seconds and check: if there are still large pieces of paper visible, allow another ten seconds and check it again. Do not worry about little bits that do not break down entirely, as they can add character to the paper.

If you do not have a blender, you can beat the soaked paper strips into pulp by pounding them in a bucket with a thick stick or bottle filled with water. Although pounding the pulp is historically more authentic than using electric appliances, it is hard work, and time-consuming.

As you make the pulp, pour it into a bucket or large plastic bottle until you have enough for several sheets. Approximately one load in the blender will make one thin sheet of A4 (297 x 210 mm) paper or a slightly thicker sheet of A5 paper (210 x 148 mm). You will have to experiment to determine which thickness you prefer. If the pulp is too thick, simply add more water, but do not dilute it too much as this will produce fine, fragile sheets which may be difficult to work with until you are more experienced.

Torn strips of paper are soaked in water before being macerated in the blender.

Note: Be careful not to beat the pulp for too long. A good way to test whether the pulp has been beaten enough, is to put a teaspoon of beaten pulp into a jar of water. Seal the lid and shake the jar. If you can see individual fibres floating in the water, the pulp has reached the right consistency. If there are still clumps or whole pieces left, it must be blended a little longer. If the pulp has reached a creamy consistency with no fibres visible, it has been beaten for too long – the fibres will be too short to bond together strongly.

Pouring pulp onto felt

Lay a dry felt onto a wide tray or several sheets of newspaper. Make sure the felt is totally flat and level. Place the frame on the felt, allowing a margin of fabric all round.

Fill a 500-ml jug (or large yoghurt carton) with pulp from a bucket, and with a rapid movement of your wrist, pour the pulp over the felt within the frame. Give the underlying tray or felt a quick shake to the right and left, forwards and backwards. This disperses the fibres evenly and creates a uniform sheet of paper. Stop shaking the tray after the initial dispersion, otherwise the fibres will separate again as the water drains away. Allow the water to drain for about a minute, mopping it up outside the frame with a sponge until most of the water has drained away. Remove the frame carefully, and lay another dry piece of felt on top of the wet sheet. Press the felt down gently with the flat of your hand until it begins to absorb water. Then lay a sponge over the top felt and allow it to absorb the moisture. Wring out the sponge and repeat this process until most of the excess water has been removed. Now roll a rolling pin slowly but firmly over the covering felt – this will not only press the paper, but also remove more water. When you have removed as much excess water as possible, carefully peel the top felt off the lower one, and hang up the sheet of paper, still on the lower felt, to dry.

Pouring paper pulp onto felt inside a frame.

Pressing the wet paper with a rolling pin between two felts.

Note: Take care not to press the paper with the rolling pin too soon. If the paper is still very wet, too much pressure with the rolling pin will displace the fibres and you may tear the sheet.

It is not always necessary to use the same fabric below and above the wet sheet. The top piece can be of any cotton or woollen fabric, but bear in mind that its texture will be impressed on the surface of your paper. Cheesecloth creates a lovely surface texture on which to draw.

Storing leftover pulp

Newly made or leftover pulp can be stored in sealed bottles or buckets for a few weeks. If it starts to smell, add a few drops of formalin (a solution of formaldehyde), oil of cloves or oil of wintergreen (available from any chemist) to each litre of pulp to stop the decaying process. Ordinary household bleach (about 5 ml is the right amount for a 2 ℓ bottle of pulp) can also be used. Before using the pulp again, however, you must rinse it very thoroughly. Pour it through a drainage bag, stocking or colander lined with mesh, rinse well under a running tap and return it to a bucket or bottle, slightly diluted. Experience will tell you which consistency works best, but a general rule for the pouring method is to dilute one cup of wet, *drained* pulp with one to two cups of water, depending on the thickness of paper required. If the pulp is too thick, you may get lumpy sheets.

To facilitate storing, you can drain excess pulp through mesh to reduce its bulk and then store it in the refrigerator in a sealed plastic bag. Dilute it as explained above before use. If you want to store pulp indefinitely, drain it through a stocking and hang it up to dry. When you need some, simply break off pieces of the dried material, soak it in water for an hour and blend again.

Pulp can be stored wet or dry.

PROJECT 1
Two sheets of plain paper

REQUIREMENTS
Basic equipment list (see p 16)
Small embroidery or picture frame
Five facial tissues or two serviettes
500 ml of boiling water
Four pieces of cotton fabric
Iron and ironing board
Tray

Tear the tissues into strips, place these in a jug and add the boiling water. Leave to stand for about ten minutes. Lay a handkerchief or a piece of cotton fabric on the tray, making sure that the material is flat and the tray level. Position the frame centrally on the fabric. Blend the tissues and water in the blender for five seconds (or beat it with an egg beater) to a creamy pulp. In the meantime, switch on the iron, setting it to medium heat.

Now quickly pour the blended pulp onto the fabric inside the frame and shake the tray to disperse the fibres. Allow the water to drain for about a minute, mopping it up outside the frame with a sponge. Lay the second piece of fabric on top (covering both pulp and frame) and continue mopping until most of the water has drained away. Lift the top layer of fabric and carefully remove the frame. Replace the top piece of fabric and gently roll a rolling pin over the paper 'sandwich'. Then carefully peel off the top piece of fabric and replace it with a dry one. Smooth it down well and begin ironing until the fabric feels dry. Turn the paper 'sandwich' over and peel away the remaining piece of wet fabric. Replace it with dry fabric and iron until it feels dry. Continue ironing on both sides until the paper is bone-dry, and peel off one of the pieces of fabric. Insert a knife under a corner of the paper to lift an edge, turn the paper face down, and peel the other piece of fabric away from it.

The wet sheet of paper can be ironed dry between two pieces of fabric.

PROJECT 2
Two sheets of mottled paper

Mottled paper is made by mixing two different kinds of pulp. Make one cup of coloured tissue pulp, and one cup of plain pulp. To prepare the latter, tear wastepaper such as notepaper, envelopes or computer paper into small pieces and add boiling water. Leave to stand for an hour and then macerate in a blender for 20 seconds. Proceed as for Project 1, but pour the plain and coloured pulp into the frame simultaneously. As you shake the tray, the pulp will blend together, forming a mottled sheet of paper. Iron dry as before.

Opposite: Equipment and paper from Project 1.

Right: Papers from Projects 1 and 2.

Chapter 3
Making paper with a mould

The mould with its newly formed sheet of paper is left to drain over the vat.

Now that you have made your first few sheets of paper, you will have gained some understanding of the properties and possibilities of paper pulp. When broken down and mixed with water, plant fibres will bond together to form paper. (In the case of recycling, the fibres used will usually be those of wood pulp.)

The method of paper-making described in this chapter is the most common, and bears the closest resemblance to the process used both traditionally and in modern industry. The pulp is suspended in water in a container called a vat, in the ratio of 2-5 per cent pulp to 95-98 per cent water. A screen known as a paper-maker's mould is lowered into the vat and lifted out of the pulp. The water drains through the screen and leaves a thin layer of pulp on the mesh. This 'wet sheet' is transferred onto a piece of fabric called a felt and the process repeated until there is a pile of felts which can then be pressed. The felts with their sheets of paper are then removed individually to dry.

The following equipment is needed for this method of paper-making:

The mould

The mould is the most important piece of equipment for the paper-maker. It consists of a simple rectangular frame with mesh stretched across it to form a sieve for the pulp.

The moulds of professional paper-makers are usually made with mahogany frames and brass wire mesh, with strong joints able to stand up to years of immersion in water. It is also customary to have two moulds to each deckle, which makes it possible for one mould to drain while the other is dipped into the vat containing the pulp. For the amateur it is, however, possible to make paper with simpler and less expensive moulds.

Improvised moulds

❏ A simple round mould can be made by stretching nylon net curtaining over an embroidery frame.
❏ A flat wire sieve (such as a spatter shield) can also be used to form round sheets.
❏ A picture frame with net curtaining stapled onto it will work well for small sheets. A picture frame of the same size, with the net omitted, can be used as a 'deckle' (see p 26).

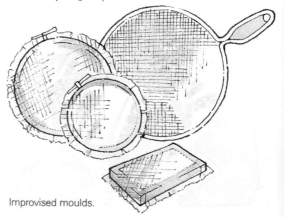

Improvised moulds.

The paper-maker's mould

A more durable but simple frame can be made from wood. The inside dimensions of the frame will be determined by the size of the paper you wish to make. The measurements for two frame sizes are given below.

> **Note:** *With the exception of the first five projects, the measurements and quantities referred to in this book apply to making A4 sheets of paper. This is the standard size widely used for business stationery, brochures and printing. The A system follows the ISO (International Standards Organization) system of sizing paper. A4 paper measures 297 x 210 mm; doubling A4 will produce A3, and halving A4 will produce A5. A5 is generally used for leaflets and small booklets and can be made by roughly halving the given quantities.*

1. To make sheets of A4 paper, the inside area of the frame will measure 300 x 210 mm. Strips of wood for the frame should measure 20 x 50 mm. You will need two pieces 210 mm long and two pieces 340 mm long, simply glued and nailed together at the corners. The corners can be further reinforced with brass L-shaped braces.

2. To make paper approximately A5 in size, the inside dimensions of the frame will be 210 x 150 mm. The strips of wood should measure 20 x 20 mm and you will need two pieces 150 mm long, and two pieces 250 mm long.

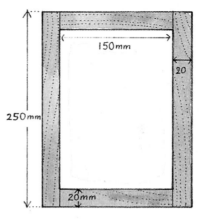

Dimensions for a mould to make an A5 size sheet.

When the frame is finished, it must be covered with mesh, stretched as taut as possible. The mesh can be pinned or stapled to the frame. Materials that can be used as mesh include net curtaining, fly-screen or mosquito mesh, silk-screen mesh, or any porous fabric with a fine gauge. If you use fabric, wet it before stretching, as some kinds tend to sag when placed in water, resulting in sheets of paper of uneven thickness. When making the mould, avoid using ferrous metals, as this will cause foxing and ruin the paper. Foxing is the brownish rust stain which develops when pulp or paper comes into contact with metal objects.

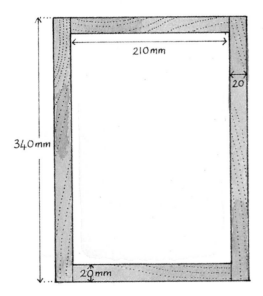

Dimensions for a mould to make an A4 size sheet.

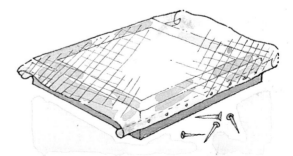

The mesh is stretched taut as it is nailed to the frame.

Irregular deckle-edges characteristic of handmade paper.

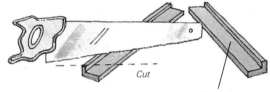

Picture framing

Saw the moulding with the help of a mitre box and fasten it at the corners so that it rests quite firmly on the mould. The corners may be reinforced with brass L-shaped braces and the joints glued with woodglue for further strength.

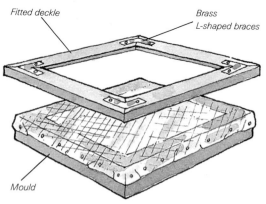

Fitted deckle

Brass L-shaped braces

Mould

The deckle

The deckle, a removable open frame the same size as the mould, rests on top of the mesh and contains the pulp within the surface area of the screen. This determines the size of the sheet of paper to be formed, and causes the irregular deckle-edge so characteristic of handmade paper. Without the deckle, the paper will be thinner and the edge more irregular.

For a simple but perfectly adequate deckle, make a second frame identical to the mould but only 25 mm deep and omit the mesh.

A more sophisticated deckle to fit snugly onto the mould will require a bit of carpentry. It can be constructed from picture frame moulding of 30 mm wide, including a flange of about 5 mm wide. You will need approximately 1,5 m for a deckle to fit an A4 mould (this allows for waste during cutting).

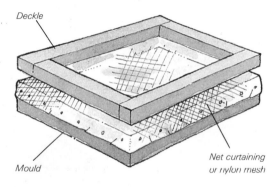

Deckle

Mould

Net curtaining or nylon mesh

The vat

The vat is a large container for holding the water and pulp with which the paper is made. It must be large enough to accommodate the mould and deckle held in both hands. A plastic baby bath with a capacity of about 20 ℓ of water is perfect for making A4 sheets, while a square washing-up bowl (with a capacity of about 12 ℓ) will be fine for making smaller sheets of paper such as A5. For making larger sheets of paper on a larger mould, you can use a water storage tank, tote box (from restaurant suppliers) or a chemical drum cut in half.

Felt

The wet sheets of paper are transferred from the mould onto absorbent fabric, traditionally felted woollen cloth (*see* p 16).

Forming the paper with a mould

A bucket of prepared pulp (about 8 ℓ) will make 20 to 25 sheets of thinnish A4 paper. You will have to experiment with the thickness you require, but start off by pouring 3 ℓ of pulp into a baby bath and add cold water up to about 70 mm from the top.

Before you begin, agitate the pulp in the vat by stirring it gently with your hand or a wooden spoon. This must be done before forming each sheet, as the pulp tends to settle on the bottom. Do not stir too wildly, as too much turbulence in the vat will result in paper with lumps and ridges. Dampen the mesh on the mould before forming your first sheet, to facilitate drainage of the pulp.

Facing the vat, hold the mould with both hands by the short sides and lower it vertically into the far side of the vat. Then gently tilt the mould towards you until it is lying horizontally, about 50 mm below the surface of the water. Be careful not to bump the sides of the vat with the mould, as this causes ridges. Gradually lift the mould, holding it level, and allow it to drain over the vat for about 15 seconds, until most of the water has drained away. Then tilt it slightly to drain for another ten seconds. If you have two moulds, you could put the one aside to drain while you form another sheet with the other. After every two or three sheets, top up the vat with 1 ℓ of pulp.

If you are unhappy with a sheet, simply invert the mould and lower it onto the pulp in the vat. When the pulp has fallen from the mould, stir the pulp in the vat well and dip the mould again.

Using a deckle

Hold the deckle against the mould with your thumbs on top and fingers underneath as you immerse both frames in the vat. Lift them out of the vat and as they clear the surface but before the water drains away, give the mould (and deckle) a gentle shake backwards, forwards and sideways to disperse the fibres. Relax as you do this, moving from the shoulders and not just the wrists. Then drain the wet sheet in the same way as when using a mould. After about 30 seconds you should be able to remove the deckle gently. Be very careful not to let any drops fall on the wet sheet – these will form little spots of thinner pulp, or 'water marks'.

> **Note:** As a general rule, you will need slightly less pulp in the vat when forming sheets with a deckle than without. Start with 2½ ℓ and top up as you proceed.

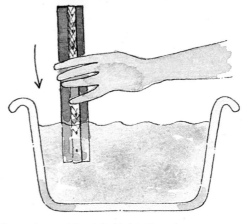

Lower the mould and deckle into the vat.

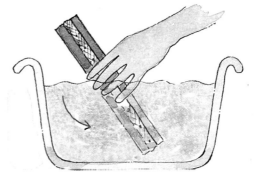

Tilt the mould towards you while it is still submerged under water.

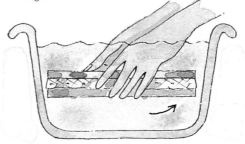

Lift the mould out of the water and give it a shake.

Drying a sheet on the mould

At this point, you can simply tilt the frame on its side and leave it to dry. It will dry much quicker outside in the sun, or next to a heater. On a windy or sunny day, the paper will dry in a couple of hours.

In sunny weather and with two moulds in operation, it is possible to make up to 12 sheets a day using this method. Strong winds can, however, topple the mould and ruin the paper. To prevent this, the mould may be leant against a flower pot in a sunny position with a brick or heavy stone placed at the base to hold it firm. Be careful, too, of rain or garden sprinklers, as any water falling on the wet pulp will displace the fibres and create holes. Furthermore do not leave your paper outside overnight, as snails will make short work of it. To remove the paper from the mould, slide a sharp knife under a corner of the paper and work it along the top edge to loosen it. Then gently peel off the paper.

The couching method

The term 'couch' probably comes from the French verb *coucher*, meaning 'to lay down'. After forming a wet sheet on a mould and allowing it to drain sufficiently, you can couch it onto a piece of wet felt.

First, create a small pile of about five to six *wet* felts to form a soft pad to facilitate couching. Without this pad, the first few sheets could be formed badly. A wet folded towel or wet piece of carpet underfelt may also be placed underneath the pad of felts to create a suitable mound. After creating a pile of about ten sheets of paper, the towel or underfelt should be removed – the pile of wet felts and paper will be sufficient.

Rest the mould with the long left-hand side of the frame against the right-hand side of the felt, with the wet paper facing to the left. Hold the mould vertically, so that your left hand holds the raised left side of the frame. Using both hands and a gentle rolling

The paper can be left on the mould and dried outside in the sun.

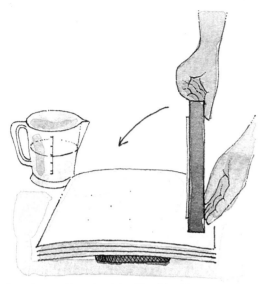

Rest the mould on the right side of the felt, pulp facing left.

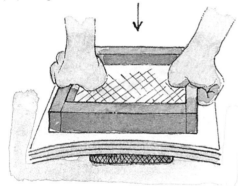

Roll the mould firmly against the felt from right to left in a smooth rocking motion.

Lift the mould on the right, leaving the wet sheet on the felt.

motion, lower the mould (pulp against the felt) down flat on the felt with your left hand, and lift it up with the right. While the motion should be smooth, the pressure should be sufficient to transfer the wet pulp onto the felt. Press the mould quite firmly if you are unsure to begin with. With practice you should soon be able to do this in one smooth, fairly rapid movement. Do not be disheartened if the first sheet is not successful, as it often causes problems. Place another wet felt on top of the first sheet of paper, and couch a second sheet onto this. Continue in this manner until you have a substantial pile of felts and paper. The pile should then be pressed.

The professional couching method is to build up what is known as a post of felts (144 sheets), which is then pressed. For the amateur working at home, a good number is between 20 and 50 sheets. This will, however, be determined by the number of felts you have (see Chapter 4 for pressing and drying a post of felts).

It is important to have the correct amount of moisture in the felts. They must be quite damp, but not sopping wet. This comes with practice, but as a general rule for the beginner, they should rather be too wet than too dry.

The couching of pulp from right to left is not a rigid rule and if you are left-handed you may want to try it the other way round. Some people also couch from back to front, rolling the mould toward them. Experiment to find the method you find most comfortable.

> **Note:** It is possible to couch sheets of paper onto vilene (non-iron dressmakers' vilene), handkerchiefs, pieces of cotton or silk and then iron them dry. Simply wet a piece of thinner fabric of your choice, place it on a wet pile of felts and couch as usual. To iron, follow the method described in Project 1. Bear in mind that the texture of the fabric will be reflected in the texture of the sheet of paper. Thinner fabrics are unsuitable when hanging the paper up to dry as the paper tends to curl badly (or cockle, as it is generally known), particularly in the case of bigger sheets. To keep the paper from curling, remove it from the fabric just before it has dried completely and press it between blotting paper, replacing the blotting paper with dry sheets when it becomes damp. Store the paper in a heavy book for a week.

PROJECT 3
Round sheet of paper, ironed dry

REQUIREMENTS
*Small embroidery frame (150 mm in
    diameter) with net curtaining stretched
    across it*
*Mixing bowl or plastic container large
    enough for immersed frame*
1 ℓ of prepared pulp
*Iron, ironing board and two handkerchiefs
    for ironing*

Pour 500 ml of the pulp into the bowl and top
it up with water to about 25 mm below the
rim. Wet the mesh on the frame by dipping it
upside down in the bowl. Holding the frame
with both hands on either side with the
mesh facing you, lower it vertically into the
bowl. Gradually tilt it horizontally towards
you, making sure it is well below the surface
of the water. Slowly lift the frame, giving it a
slow shake in all directions as it reaches the
surface. Lift it above the water and allow it to
drain for about 20 seconds. Gently remove
the net from the frame, cover with a dry
handkerchief and iron dry as in Project 1
(*see* p 21), peeling the net from the back of
the paper when bone-dry. Leave the rest of
the pulp in the bowl for Project 4.

PROJECT 4
Round sheet of paper, air-dried
on the frame

Pour the rest of the pulp into the bowl. Using
the same embroidery frame, form a wet sheet
in the bowl as for Project 3 and allow it to
drain for ten seconds. Then, in a warm spot,
tilt the frame on its side and allow the paper
to dry completely. To remove, simply insert a
sharp knife under a corner of the paper, work
it around the edge, and peel the paper off the
net. Press it in a heavy book for a week.

Opposite: Finished papers from Projects 3 and 4. One
sheet is left to dry on the frame.

Right: A round sheet of paper couched onto a wet
handkerchief laid over a damp pad.

PROJECT 5
Couching two sheets of paper

REQUIREMENTS
*Same as for Project 3, plus
Three handkerchiefs
Towel
Two dishcloths*

First make a small pad with a folded towel
and two dishcloths and wet them well. Make
sure they are well smoothed out, with no
bubbles trapped between the layers of fabric.
Lay a wet handkerchief on top and smooth
down as before. Using the method explained
in Project 3, form a sheet of paper on an
embroidery frame and couch it onto a
handkerchief in a smooth rolling motion. Lay
the handkerchief and its wet paper on
newspaper for half an hour and then hang it
up to dry. Repeat for the second sheet.
Remove the paper from the handkerchief
before it is completely dry and press it
between blotting paper, replacing the blotting
paper with dry sheets when it becomes
damp. Press the paper in a heavy book for
a week.

> **Note:** *You can also use a small picture frame
> with net curtain stapled onto it, or if you
> already have an A5 mould, you can pour
> 1½ ℓ of pulp into a kitchen sink, top it up
> with water, and form and couch two sheets
> of paper as described above.*

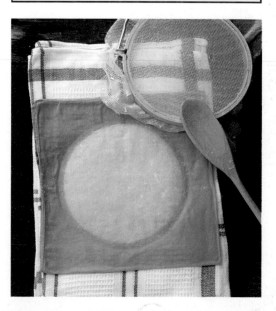

Chapter 4
Pressing and drying paper

Various pressing methods

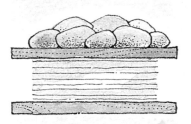

Simple pressing method

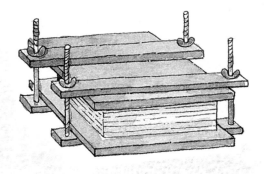

Early pressing method

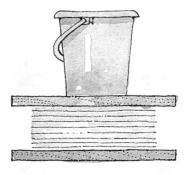

Simple pressing method

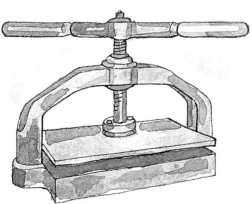

Simple screw press

Pressing is necessary both before and after drying sheets of paper. The purpose of pressing a post of wet sheets on felt is to bond the fibres firmly and remove as much excess water as possible before separating the felts for drying. This also speeds up the drying process and prevents the paper from curling or cockling. Pressing the dry paper will flatten and smooth it.

Early pressing methods in the East were simple, employing pressing boards and heavy rocks piled on top of the post, or a simple lever press with weights hung on the end of a pole. Pressure was gradually increased over several hours. Western paper-makers, on the other hand, traditionally pressed their post of felts in wooden screw presses tightened by means of a long wooden lever. Today Western mills making handmade paper use powerful hydraulic presses which can exert a pressure of between 100 and 150 tons. Although most Japanese paper-makers today also use screw or hydraulic presses, the emphasis still falls on gradually applying pressure rather than rapidly as is the case in the West. This is worth bearing in mind when making paper from plants.

Bookbinder's press

Pressing paper

The simplest method of pressing a pile of felts is to sandwich it between two boards and to stand on it for ten minutes. The heavier you are, the more effective the method. To continue the pressure, stack bricks on the board and leave it for a couple of hours. Alternatively, place a large bucket on top and fill it with water or sand.

A simple press can be made with two pieces of hardwood (or varnished pine to avoid warping) larger than the felts, clamped with four strips of wood and carriage bolts.

Once you have a post of felts, transfer it to the press and screw down the carriage bolts. If you turn the press on its side and leave it to stand vertically on a sink or draining board, it takes about half an hour for most of the excess water to drain. You can then separate the felts for drying.

If you are lucky enough to get hold of a bookbinder's press, it will be perfect for pressing paper. Simply slide in the felts (sandwiched between boards) and screw down the press until you have applied a fair amount of pressure. After about 10 minutes, give the lever another turn to increase the pressure. Leave the pile in the press for about half an hour before removing it.

Separating the felts

After opening the press, peel away the top felt to reveal the first wet sheet of paper. Each felt with its wet sheet must be separated from the one below and dried individually. To separate the felts, peel them apart carefully, gently lifting a corner without lifting the sheet below. If the sheet below begins lifting, lower the felt and try another edge. This process cannot be hurried.

Drying the paper

It is advisable to dry couched paper indoors, away from wind, sun or rain. If it dries too quickly or unevenly, the edges will cockle. Felts can be pegged on an indoor drying line over a bath, or on a clotheshorse standing on newspapers to catch the drips.

Alternatively you can lay the individual felts down flat on newspaper, although this takes up a lot of space. It is also preferable to let the air circulate around the felts. In warm weather and dry climates, the paper should be dry in one or two days. In winter it will take longer. To speed up the drying process, lay the wet sheets (on their felts) down flat on sheets of newspaper for a few hours prior to hanging them up. When the felts feel dry to the touch, the sheets of paper can be removed.

Removing the paper from the felt

To remove the dry paper from the felt, first slide a sharp knife under a corner of the paper and work the knife along the top edge to loosen it. Then turn the felt over so that the paper is face down (on a clean, dry surface) and gently peel the felt away from the paper. When the felts have been used for some time, this process becomes easier. At first, you may have to work the knife around the entire edge of the paper until it comes away cleanly.

Once you have removed the paper from the felts, press them in a heavy book for a week. Alternatively, interleave them with stiff card and press them between pressing boards weighted down with bricks. If you have a screw or hydraulic press, 24 hours of pressure should be sufficient. As the paper is still unsized (i.e. no substance has been added to it to make it less absorbent) you can at this stage write on the paper only with ballpoint or pencil, not ink.

Couched paper on felts hanging up to dry.

Removing dried paper from felt with a knife.

How to make a 'weight brick'

A useful piece of equipment for both the hand-papermaker and the bookbinder is a weight brick. Find a smooth brick and wrap it (like a parcel) with two sheets of newspaper. Secure the newspaper tightly with adhesive tape, and then cover the whole with a layer of coloured or decorative paper. To press your (dry) paper, cards, envelopes or book, stack it between two boards and place the brick on top.

Wrap a brick tightly in two layers of newspaper.

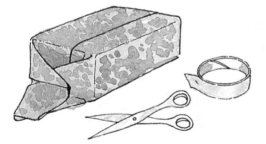

Wrap the covered brick with decorative paper.

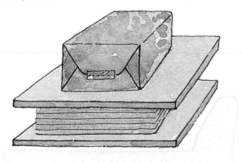

Press dry paper between boards under the brick.

Opposite: Wet sheets on their felts, laid on newspapers to dry.

Above right: A post of felts and paper, couched one on top of the other.

PROJECT 6
Couching a post of ten sheets of A4 paper

For this project you will need to invest in a few items of equipment and make a larger quantity of pulp than previously.

REQUIREMENTS
Basic equipment (see p 16)
15 felts
A4 mould
6 ℓ of white pulp

To tint the pulp slightly, make a pot of tea and add the liquid to the pulp in the bucket. Stir it in well and leave the pulp to stand for an hour. Then pour 3 ℓ of prepared pulp into the vat and top up with water. Using a mould without a deckle, form ten sheets of paper and couch them onto wet felts, one on top of the other, until you have a post (*see p 28* for instructions on couching). Remember to add 1 ℓ of pulp to the tub after every two to three sheets. Press the post, using one of the methods described above, before separating the felts and hanging them up to dry. When dry, remove the sheets from the felts and press them under weights or in a heavy book for a week.

Rosebank 7700

14 Februa[ry]

es St.

Dear Letta

you for the beautiful photograph
yourself— I will treasure it. It will
ook good in a brass frame—possibly
backed with home-made paper.
our own sheets are almost dry now
and will be put in the press for 24
hours to flatten them, and thereafter
will be stored under weights for a
week or two. I have sized them, so
you will be able to write on them.

— Have fun, and lots of love

Marianne

The healing comes when we stop fighting the condition

JOEL GOLDSMITH

Faye Collins
12 Denver Place,
2040 Honeydew.

Chapter 5
Preparing a writing surface

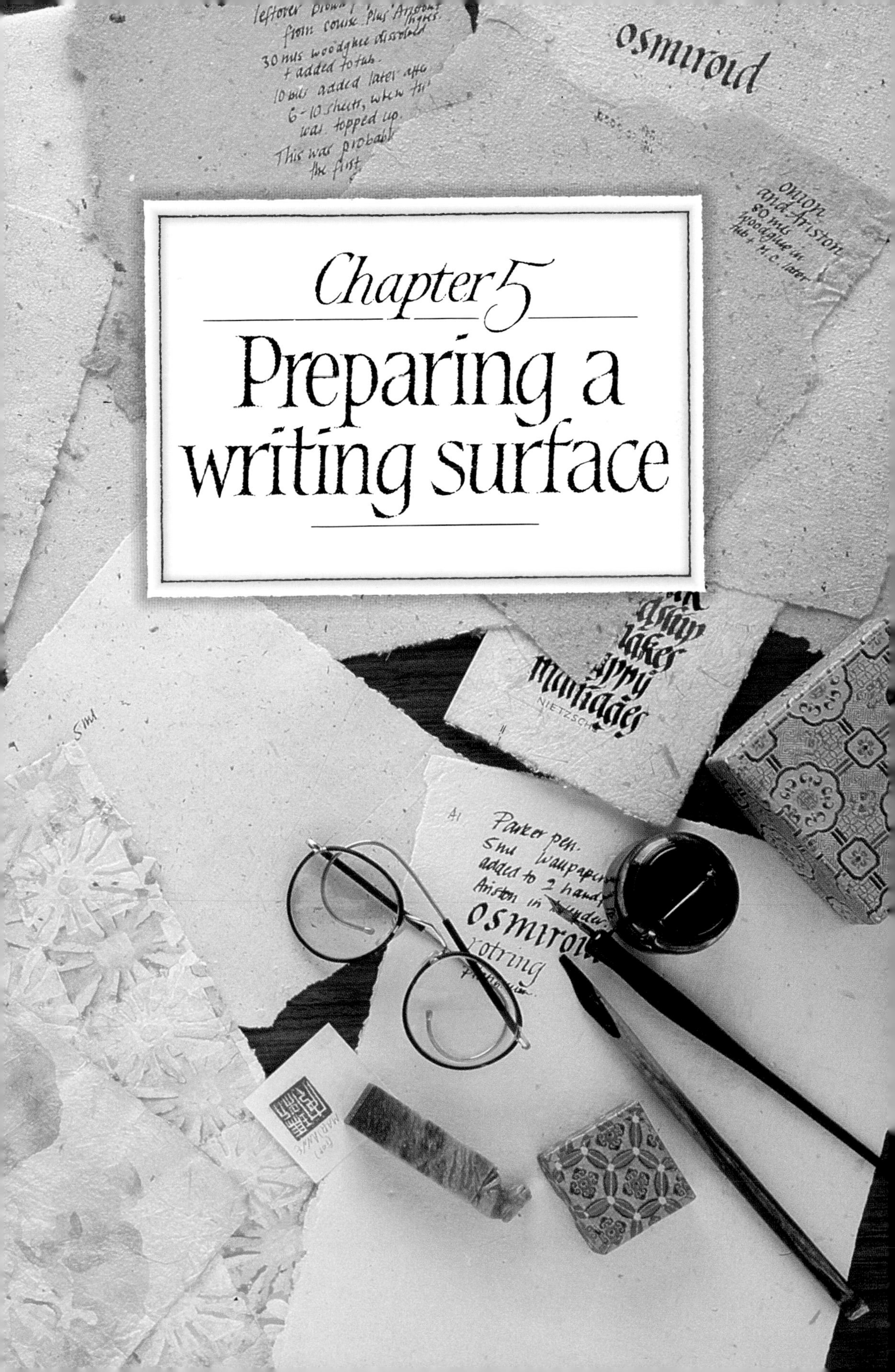

In order to be able to write on paper with ink, the paper must be sized, that is, a glue-like substance must be added to the paper to render it less absorbent. Sizing also strengthens paper. Unsized paper is good for printing and lino-cuts, and you can write on it with ballpoint or pencil, but you can not use calligraphy inks. If the paper is unsized, the ink will bleed, as it does when you write on blotting paper or tissue. Papers in the East are traditionally unsized because wood blocks were originally used for printing and only one side of the paper was used. Western printing methods, however, demanded a well-sized opaque paper, suitable for printing on both sides without showing through. Gelatine sizing was traditionally used before being replaced by chemical methods of sizing.

The following sizing methods are simple and the ingredients available in most supermarkets. The methods either entail sizing the paper after it has dried, or adding a sizing substance to pulp in a vat. All quantities given for the latter apply to a bucket of prepared pulp (about 8 ℓ). Approximate measurements are given, as a handful of soaked paper used to make one load of pulp in a blender varies from person to person. The quantity of size will alter accordingly and minor adjustments may have to be made to suit your needs. It is always advisable to write down all your experiments in a notebook so that you can repeat successful ones and adjust unsuccessful ones. You are encouraged to experiment and find the method that gives you the best results for your requirements.

Gelatine sizing is historically one of the most popular sizing methods in the West because of its inherent stability and neutral pH. It also produces an excellent surface for calligraphy inks. Dissolve 4,5 ml of gelatine in 250 ml of boiling water, and use a wide, soft paintbrush to paint it onto dry paper still on its felt. After sizing the paper, hang it up again to dry. Sizing it twice with less concentrated gelatine (approximately 3 ml to 250 ml water) is sometimes better than one sizing, as there will be less risk of streaking or bubbling.

The above quantity will size about ten sheets. Mixing more is impractical, as the gelatine begins to cool and set after a few sheets. The disadvantage of this method is

that the gelatine has to be hot, and the sizing can only be done after the paper has dried. Also, the paper will be more effectively sized on one side than the other.

Use a soft paintbrush to size the paper with a gelatine solution.

Note: Paper must not be too acidic or alkaline. If acids are present, the molecular structure of the cellulose in the paper breaks down, causing it to become discoloured, weak and brittle. Alkalinity and acidity can be conveniently measured with a pH indicator (a type of litmus paper) and the scale ranges from 14 (extremely alkaline) to 1 (extremely acid). Red wine, for example, has a pH of about 3½ while milk has a pH of between 6 and 7. A pH of 7 is regarded as neutral. However, exposure to the atmosphere renders any paper acidic over time, so a pH of about 8 is regarded as safer by conservationists. For this reason, it is best to avoid sizing methods that increase the acidity of the paper, such as the rosin and alum sizing frequently used by large paper-mills.

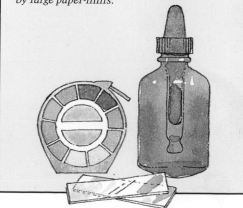

Sunlight soap makes a good size. Grate between 20-25 g (I use an accurate scale that measures grams) of soap and dissolve it in a jug of boiling water. When cool, it sets into a jelly, which is then further diluted in boiling water. Add this to the pulp in a bucket, stirring it in well. Couch or air-dry the paper as explained previously. It forms a beautiful surface to write on, but for long-lasting papers the pH might be suspect.

Starch can be used on its own, or in conjunction with another sizing method such as gelatine. Dissolve 20 ml in a little cold water, stir it into a jug of boiling water until it thickens and add it to the pulp in a bucket (about 8 ℓ). It produces paper with a pleasant surface to write on and when you shake the sheet, you will hear a firm rattling sound. For calligraphy inks the paper will need further sizing (3,7 ml of gelatine in 250 ml of boiling water, painted on with a soft watercolour brush). Increasing the amount of starch in order to size the paper in one operation is not successful, as the pulp thickens and becomes less manageable in the vat. The water also takes longer to drain through the mesh.

Woodglue (25 ml of glue dissolved in a jug of boiling water) can be added to the pulp in a bucket. For calligraphy inks a second sizing with gelatine (3,7 ml of gelatine dissolved in 250 ml of boiling water) will improve the surface. Woodglue produces paper with a good writing surface and a firm rattling sound when shaken, but the pH is suspect.

Methyl cellulose (low substitution powder) can be obtained from chemical suppliers in amounts of 500 g. Although this method of sizing is expensive and not as readily available as those listed above, it is excellent because of its stability and neutral pH. It must be made up at least 24 hours before use, as it takes a while to dissolve.

Dissolve 15 ml in a little water until it forms a thick jelly, then gradually dilute it until you have 2 ℓ of solution. Methyl cellulose is convenient because it has a long shelf life and can be sprayed onto dry paper with a small spray gun, producing an excellent surface for calligraphy. A good drenching – the paper may be quite wet after spraying – will ensure that the paper is well sized.

Spraying a solution of methyl cellulose onto paper in order to size it.

PROJECT 7
Sizing tinted paper in two operations

REQUIREMENTS
Basic equipment (see p 16)
A4 mould and deckle
6 ℓ of prepared pulp
Household starch
Gelatine
Wide, soft paintbrush
Two sheets of brightly coloured paper

Shred two sheets of coloured paper and pour boiling water over the shreds. Leave to stand for 15 minutes and then blend small handfuls for seven seconds at a time. Add this mixture to the 6 ℓ of pulp.

Dissolve 15 ml of household starch in a little cold water, stir in boiling water until it thickens and add it to the pulp. Mix well and leave to stand for an hour. Pour 2½ ℓ of the pulp-and-starch mixture into a vat, topping up with water. Using a mould and deckle, form and couch ten sheets of paper in the usual manner. Press the post and hang the felts up to dry.

To size the dry sheets still on their felts, dissolve 3,7 ml of gelatine in 250 ml of boiling water, stirring well until all gelatine globules have dissolved. Use a wide, soft brush to paint on the gelatine solution from left to right. Hang up the sheets of paper to dry – this should take about 24 hours. Remove the sheets from the felts and press them in a heavy book for a week or two. Alternatively, stack them between sheets of ordinary card and place them under a board and weights for a week.

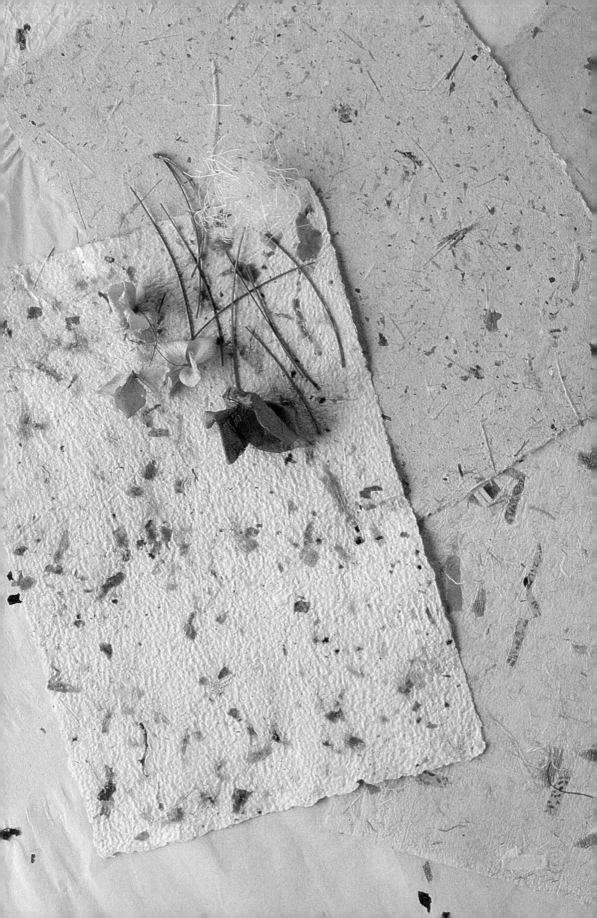

Chapter 6
Colouring and texturing paper

Colouring handmade paper can create beautiful effects in a range of colours. A simple method is to blend coloured paper and add it to the pulp. Alternatively, various natural and chemical dyes can be added to the pulp, creating subtle tints and shades of paper. The addition of textural interest in the form of petals, leaves, fabric oddments or cotton thread further enhances the handmade sheet. This chapter includes a variety of different colouring and texturing methods.

Colouring the paper

Coloured, crinkle or tissue paper can be torn up and soaked for a few hours. Add a few pieces of these to the blender when you blend the other pulp. Black paper can be added to create darker shades.

Natural dyes can be derived from tea or coffee or the liquids of boiled plant fibres, such as onion skins, berberis, bark, beetroot, privet, wandering jew or arum lily, or powdered spices, such as turmeric or ginger. Blend the pulp with the liquid or spice to mix it in well.

Powdered paint, inks or food colouring can be added in small quantities to the pulp in a blender. If you add 2 ml per blender load it will result in a pale tint, whereas 5 ml will create quite an intense colour.

Simple dyes, for example Dylon dyes bought from chemists, batik dyes or Dr Martin's dyes obtainable from hobby and art shops. Mixed according to the instructions and added to the pulp in a bucket, these dyes result in attractive colours. It is best to leave most dyes in the pulp for an hour or two before making the paper.

Textile pigments or dyes are sold in large quantities – the smallest are usually 1- or 5-kg tubs – and they are usually quite expensive. However, they go a long way, so if you need large quantities of dye, the basic textile dyes, either in powder or liquid form, are excellent. Add them to the pulp in a bucket but use them in minute quantities. Depending on the tint required, 2 ml of powdered paint will colour one sheet only, whereas the same quantity of textile pigments will colour a whole bucket of pulp.

Natural ingredients can add texture and colour.

Texturing the paper

❏ Herbs, pine needles, feathers, pieces of cotton fabric and wool and gold sewing thread can be cut into pieces and added to the pulp in a vat to cause random patterns and textures.

❏ Autumn leaves and flower heads can be boiled for 30 minutes, partially blended and added to the pulp in a vat. Be careful not to overdo it. A little added at a time will be more attractive than too much, and the paper will also be easier to write on.

❏ White or coloured paper, only partially blended, can be added to the pulp to create textural interest.

❏ Dried, pressed flowers and herbs, or ferns, feathers and crushed shells can be positioned on a wet sheet. Once pressed, this will form an embossed shape which will remain on the dry paper. Alternatively, a second sheet can be laminated on top of the first sheet to sandwich the objects in between (*see* Chapter 9 for laminating and embossing).

❏ Plant fibres can be prepared according to the instructions in Chapter 7 and added to pulp made by recycling paper.

PROJECT 8
Sizing textured paper in one operation

REQUIREMENTS
Basic equipment (see p 16)
6 ℓ of prepared pulp
Sunlight soap
Grater
Powdered paint

Add 3 ml of red, yellow or blue powdered paint to each load of pulp in the blender. Pour the pulp into a bucket. Then collect two handfuls of flowers or dried autumn leaves and boil them for 30 minutes. Place the cooked plants in the blender with three cups of water and blend for five seconds. You may need to do this in two batches. Add this to the pulp in the bucket.

Grate 15-20 g of Sunlight soap and dissolve it in a jug of boiling water. When cool, dilute it further with boiling water and add it to the pulp. Stir the soap into the pulp with a wooden spoon, mixing it well. Allow to stand for 30 minutes.

Place 2 ℓ of pulp in a vat. Use a mould and deckle to form 15-20 sheets and couch them as usual. Top up the vat with pulp after every two sheets. Press the post of sheets and hang the felts up to dry. When dry, the paper should be sized well enough to take most calligraphy inks. Press the sheets in a heavy book or under weights for at least a week before using them.

Materials and finished papers from Project 8.

Chapter 7

Making paper from plants

Paper made from plants has a textural quality that is visually and sensuously beautiful. The smell of some plants lingers in the paper long after it has been made, reminiscent of gardens and meadows in the heat of summer. Fine plant paper resembles Japanese paper in its translucency and strength and feels quite different from paper made by recycling. Even adding plant fibres to recycled paper will enhance its attractiveness and durability. The pleasure of looking for suitable plant materials and processing them for paper-making can lead to an increased interest in botany, ecology and chemistry. Each plant species will respond differently according to the time it is picked, the season, its growing conditions and the method of processing. The sensitive handling of plant fibres becomes important when one attempts to create fine quality paper. As you become familiar with the different plants, you will begin to appreciate the exquisite workmanship of Japanese paper-makers in making their fine, tissue-like but strong and long-lasting papers.

Almost any plant can be used to make paper, but those with long fibres are most successful. Examples of such plants include leeks, celery, spinach, gladioli, irises, day lilies, river reeds, pampas grasses, bamboo leaves, banana plants (stems and leaves), papyrus, maize, red hot pokers, and the Swiss cheese plant.

A pioneer in experiments with vegetable papers

About 200 years ago, when researchers were hunting for an economical alternative to linen and cotton fibre in the mass production of paper, a German naturalist, Dr Jacob Christian Schaffer, experimented with a variety of vegetable fibres, and published the results of his findings. His six-volume treatise includes paper samples made from potatoes, grape vines, tree moss, cabbage stalks, hemp, straw, reeds, wasps' nests, thistles and oak leaves, amongst others. Most of the samples include about one fifth cotton pulp to help bind the fibres together.

The plants were first chopped by hand or beaten by means of a homemade, hand-operated stamping machine. Tough fibres were sometimes first soaked in a stiff lime paste in order to reduce the beating time.

In order to remove some of the substances contained in vegetable fibres that are harmful to paper-making, the plant material must be broken down through decomposition in water. This is a longer process than that used for recycling paper, but well worth the effort. For the purposes of this book, this is achieved by one of the following methods:

1. Boiling the plant material in plain water for an hour or more.
2. Leaving it to rot or ferment for a few weeks and then boiling it in water.
3. Boiling it in an alkaline solution.
4. Soaking it in an alkaline solution before boiling.

Preparing plant material

Collect a bucket of plant material and cut the material into 2-4 cm lengths, using garden shears or a compost shredder. Make a note of the dry weight so that you can repeat successful experiments. Tough material can first be hammered with a mallet.

Checking the dry weight of chopped plants.

Boiling plants in water

Some common vegetables and flowers, or parts thereof, such as celery, leeks, rhubarb, carrot tops, spinach stalks, cauliflower leaves or the inner stems of arum lilies can be boiled for one to three hours: the tougher the plant, the longer the boiling period. Soaking the plants for an hour or two usually reduces the boiling time.

Once boiled, rinse the plants well through a net drainage bag or stocking. Squeeze the contents of the bag to loosen the soft plant material and keep rinsing until the water runs off clear. Then blend small handfuls of plant fibres in a blender in the same way as recycled paper. The time varies according to the toughness of the fibre – some plants will need up to a minute of blending. To save your blender, blend for 20 seconds, pause and then blend again.

Soaking or rotting plants to break down the fibres

As a general rule, soaking tougher plants for a minimum of 24 hours before boiling them will hasten the decomposition and later reduce the time needed for boiling and beating. Banana stems, river reeds or bamboo, for example, will have to be soaked for several weeks or even months. For long soaking periods, put your chopped plants into a bucket, cover them with water and seal the bucket with plastic and preferably also a lid to prevent insects from breeding in the bucket. Leave the bucket in a warm place such as a warm balcony or sunny courtyard for as long as necessary.

Some material such as mown grass can simply be hosed down in a plastic bag or bucket and then left to stand for a few months. Wet it occasionally to speed up the decaying process. Once it has reduced to about a fifth of its original volume and has become slimy and well decomposed, it can be rinsed and boiled. Boil rotted plants outside, as the smell can be quite unpleasant. Boiling grass, for example, resembles the smell in a stable and rapidly attracts flies. I use a single-plate stove with an extension lead for boiling rotted plants outside.

Boiling plants in alkaline solutions

Japanese paper-makers traditionally boiled plant fibres in a potash solution made by passing water through the ashes of reeds, hardwoods, rice, straw or buckwheat husks. Contemporary Japanese paper-makers use soda ash and occasionally lime or caustic soda for boiling plant fibres. Alkalis, and particularly caustic soda, must be handled with great care.

Soda ash (Sodium carbonate)

Boiling with soda ash is the method preferred by Japanese paper-makers, who stress the gentle processing of plant fibres and avoid caustic soda which can cause damage. Soda ash is easy and fairly safe to work with. It is not necessary to wear gloves or worry excessively about spillage and mess as is the case with caustic soda. Soda ash is also cheaper, but you may need to order it through your chemist.

Boil plants in soda ash in the ratio of 20 per cent ash to the dry weight of the plant material. A 200-g sample will therefore be boiled with 40 g of soda ash (about 50 ml), in 3 ℓ of water. Boil for four to five hours, stirring and turning the plants every half hour. To check whether the material is ready, pull the fibres apart, with and against the grain. If ready, they should separate easily. For experiments with tougher plants, rather increase the boiling time and amount of soda ash before you try caustic soda.

Leave the pot to cool before rinsing, then drain the contents through a net drainage bag, immersing the bag repeatedly in fresh buckets of water until the water runs off clear. Squeeze the bag regularly to loosen the soft plant material, leaving the fibres suitable for paper-making. Once clean, the plants can be blended into pulp and couched as usual.

Before blending, you could beat the fibres by hand for five minutes to reduce the time needed for blending, which weakens the fibres. I put drained boiled plants into a bucket and pound it with the flat end of an axe handle. In the case of some plants (e.g. papyrus), hand-beating, which results in stronger paper, may be all that is necessary. I drain the fibres and beat them on a board with the flat edge of a heavy strip of wood for 10-20 minutes.

Hand-beating cooked papyrus fibres on a board.

Caustic soda or lye (Sodium hydroxide)

Caustic soda must be treated with caution. Although the chemical is very effective in breaking down quite tough plant material, it is highly toxic to plants and animals and has a corrosive effect on most metals. It is advisable to use a stainless steel pot and to boil the plants on a small stove somewhere out of the way. If the pot boils over, the caustic soda will ultimately eat away the enamel surface of the stove. Do not boil the plants in an aluminium pot or pressure cooker. Aluminium reacts with alkalis, and when it comes into contact with caustic soda, it gives off toxic fumes and will corrode almost immediately. I know of paper-makers who have used aluminium pots with disastrous results: the caustic soda burned a hole in the pot, their plant material was all over the floor and they also had to put up with the oppressive smell of burnt fibre and caustic soda. Other paper-makers I know

A variety of papers made from papyrus.

Boiling plants outside on a small one-plate stove.

have reported massive explosions while using pressure cookers to boil plants in caustic soda.

When mixing caustic soda with water, bring the water to just under boiling point and *then* add the caustic soda. Stand back, as the caustic soda heats the water, which may bubble violently and spatter if it is too hot. Stir the solution well until the caustic soda has dissolved and only then add the plant fibres. Bring to the boil and reduce the heat to a simmer. Stir and turn the plant material in the solution every half hour, being careful not to inhale the fumes. Drain the plant material in an outside drain away from plants or pets and wear rubber gloves for protection.

The amounts of caustic soda used by paper-makers vary considerably. Taking 200 g of dry plant material and 3 ℓ of water as the basic measure, the amount varies between 20 and 40 g of caustic soda, boiled for one to six hours, depending on the toughness of the material. As a rule of thumb, it is best to use less caustic soda and to increase the boiling time rather than the other way around. Start off with 20 g (about 25 ml), boil the plants for two hours and check whether the fibres are ready. If the plant material still looks green and substantially intact, boil for another two hours. Test and repeat if necessary.

Once boiled, the contents of the pot should resemble the green slime on a stagnant pond. Allow to cool, and rinse well until the water runs off more or less clear.

Soaking plants in an alkaline solution

Soaking in an alkaline solution can reduce prolonged boiling, and on occasion replace boiling altogether. The alkaline soaking method was used by the Chinese to prepare bamboo fibres prior to stamping.

One method is to presoak the fibres in a solution of 20-30 g of caustic soda per litre of water. Place the chopped plants in a bucket and cover them with water. Mix the proportionate amount of caustic soda with a little cold water and add to the plant material in the bucket, stirring well. Cover the bucket with plastic as well as a lid and leave it in a warm place for three to six weeks, stirring daily. Then rinse the fibres well and boil them in water for two to four hours.

A safer method is to soak the plant material for a month in a solution of 30-50 g lime (calcium hydroxide) to a litre of water, stirring daily. Then rinse the fibres well and boil for two to four hours.

Bleaching the pulp

Pulp made from plants boiled in caustic soda or soda ash rarely needs further bleaching. The natural shades are attractive and unique to the individual plants. Excessive bleaching can harm the fibres and alter the pH of the paper and is therefore best avoided. However, after boiling, fresh plants tend to retain their green colour, and you may want to whiten the pulp. Add a cup of household bleach to a bucket of blended pulp and let it stand for an hour or two, stirring occasionally. Then rinse the pulp thoroughly to remove the bleach. If you want to save the bleach, drain the pulp before rinsing it.

> **Note:** *Big hand-paper mills and serious paper-makers use large, expensive Hollander beaters for breaking down cotton pulp. A Hollander looks like a large bathtub with a revolving mill wheel on one side which crushes, tears and bruises the cotton pulp against a metal bedplate as it circulates around the 'tub'. This is just not practical for the amateur at home, and the process of breaking down cotton sufficiently into suitable pulp for paper-making using simple kitchen equipment is both time-consuming and beset with difficulties. An alternative is to invent some sort of motor-driven stamping mill, which was historically one of the first successful methods used to break down cotton in Europe. Today stampers are still used in the East for breaking down fibres for Japanese paper-making.*
>
> *An important point is that the kitchen blender is not ideal as a beater, as it cuts the fibres short rather than tearing or bruising them to expose the cellulose.*

How to use a deckle-box

A deckle-box is a useful piece of equipment for making single test sheets without having to blend large quantities of pulp. This is particularly useful when you have a limited amount of pulp, or need to test whether plant fibres have been sufficiently boiled. The deckle-box is similar to the deckle in that it fits on the mould exactly, but its sides are at least 10 cm high. To use the deckle-box, first float the mould in a tub of clean water, and carefully place the deckle-box over it, with the sides fitting flush. Grasp the mould and deckle-box with both hands and push it under the water quickly to remove the air bubbles. Then beat two blender loads of plant fibres, pour the pulp into the inch or so of water inside the deckle-box and stir the pulp. When the pulp has been evenly dispersed, lift the mould and deckle-box out of the water and leave to drain. The sheet can then be couched onto wet felt or a board.

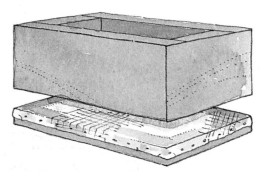

The deckle-box fits the mould exactly.

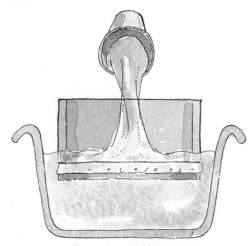

Pulp is poured into the water inside the floating deckle-box.

Note: Traditionally, Western paper was made from used linen or cotton rags, until replaced by wood pulp, which was the more plentiful and economical. Cotton has long fibres (about 2,5 mm long), a high cellulose content (about 90 per cent) and makes very good paper. Together with other plant pulps such as abaca, sisal and flax, cotton is today commercially available overseas in the form of dry compressed boards of prepared pulp (see List of Suppliers at the back of the book).

You can, however, make your own paper from old cotton or linen cloth. Boil torn rags in 2 ℓ of water and 60 g of caustic soda for 6-8 hours. Then rinse the fabric thoroughly and blend small quantities with at least three cups of water in three bursts of 20 seconds each.

Adding even a small amount of cotton to any paper will improve the quality, making it stronger, more durable and resistant to the effects of aging. If you find processing cotton too lengthy a task, you could recycle mounting-board, watercolour paper, coffee filters, photographic blotters or blotting paper and add the pulp to the plant fibres. However, bear in mind that blending cuts the fibres of recycled cotton paper and shortens them.

Couching onto a board

An alternative method to couching onto felt is to couch the paper directly onto a wooden board. Using this method you will have a dry, flat sheet in a couple of hours. It is not as difficult as it sounds. Once the mould has drained well, turn it face down onto a smooth wooden board and mop up the excess water from the underside of the mesh (the part that is now uppermost) until you can feel the paper is barely damp. Then lift the mould, revealing the paper adhering cleanly to the wooden surface. The board and paper can now be left to dry. In the case of some fibres (such as papyrus or iris) it is possible to dry these sheets in the sun, but high-shrinkage pulps (such as leeks or spinach) tend to curl off the board in strong heat. To be on the safe side, dry the paper indoors if you are unsure of its properties.

Opposite: Plant papers from top to bottom: spinach, pineapple tops, rotted grass, sisal, bamboo and dyed flower petals, unbeaten papyrus, river reed and banana leaves.

From left to right: leek, siberian iris, celery, maize, papyrus, banana leaf, river reed and day lily.

Plants suitable for paper-making

Suitable plants include the leaves and stems of various long-fibred plants. Some of these involve time-consuming stripping of bark or lengthy beating with sophisticated equipment and are beyond the scope of this book. Listed below is a broad selection of plants which provide good paper-making fibres that can be processed at home by boiling in either soda ash or caustic soda, and beating by hand or with a kitchen blender. In some cases, the tough outer part of the stem or leaves will have to be scraped or peeled before cooking and beating.

Common name	Botanical name	Strip or scrape outer skin	Blend	Handbeat
Bamboo	*Phyllostachys aurea*		✓	
Banana	*Musa nana*		✓	
Canna lily	*Canna indica*	✓	✓	
Common reed	*Phragmites communis*		✓	
Great reedmace	*Typha latifolia*		✓	
Iris	*Iris*	✓	✓	
Job's tears	*Coix lachruma*			✓
Maize stalks and husks	*Zea mays*		✓	
Mother-in-law's tongue	*Sansevieria trifasciata*	✓	✓	
New Zealand flax	*Phormium tenax*	✓	✓	
Pampas grass	*Cortaderia selloana*		✓	
Papyrus	*Cyperus papyrus*		✓	✓
Pineapple	*Ananas comosus*	✓	✓	
Sisal	*Agave sisalana*	✓	✓	
Strelitzia	*Strelitzia nicolai*		✓	
Sugar-cane	*Saccharum officinarum*		✓	
Swiss cheese plant	*Monstera deliciosa*		✓	
Wheat straw	*Triticum aestivum*		✓	
Yucca	*Yucca filamentosa*	✓	✓	

PROJECT 9
Ten sheets of onion-skin paper

REQUIREMENTS
5 ℓ of prepared plain pulp
Four to six handfuls of onion skins
Starch

Soak the onion skins for an hour and then boil them for three hours. Allow to cool and blend as usual, using the water the onion skins were boiled in. Then add the onion pulp to the prepared pulp in a bucket. Mix 12 ml of household starch in a little cold water, add to the pulp and stir well. Leave to stand for an hour, stirring occasionally. Pour 2 ℓ of pulp into a vat, form and couch the sheets as usual and hang the felts up to dry. When dry, size the paper with gelatine if you want to write on it with calligraphy ink.

PROJECT 10
Maize paper

REQUIREMENTS
250 g maize husks
4,5 ℓ of water
Cast-iron, enamel or stainless steel pot
* (minimum capacity 6 ℓ)*
50 g soda ash (about 63 ml)

Chop up the maize husks into pieces about 20 mm long and soak them in a covered bucket which is situated in a warm place for one week. Rinse the maize husks well and then boil them very gently in soda ash and water for five hours, stirring occasionally. Leave the pot to stand until the pulp is cool and then rinse it thoroughly. Follow the usual procedure for beating and forming the pulp into paper and size if required.

Maize and onion-skin papers.

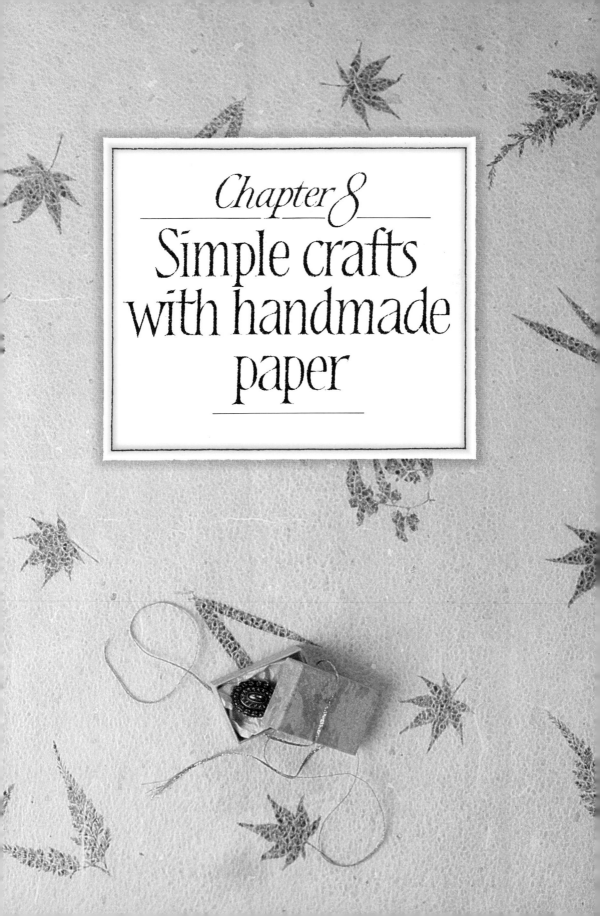

Chapter 8
Simple crafts with handmade paper

Once you have accumulated a variety of sheets of handmade paper, you may want to use them in creative ways as gifts for family or friends. A letter written on handmade paper and sent in a matching envelope is an object of beauty that can be treasured for years, and a pack of ten sheets of paper with matching envelopes is a beautiful gift. By folding handmade paper you can create original cards for special occasions such as christenings, weddings or Valentine's day. In addition, interesting bags, boxes and other containers for gifts can be made from textured handmade paper. The charm of these containers is that no two will be alike.

For most of the crafts in the following two chapters, a few basic items of equipment will be needed.

Bone folder
Hobby or craft knife
Steel ruler
Thick card for cutting on
Set square
Pencil
Glue
Scissors
Double-sided tape (from stationers)

Notepaper and cards with matching envelopes.

Notepaper and envelopes

Envelopes are made in exactly the same way as sheets of paper, using a mould and deckle and couching as explained in Chapter 3. Part of the mesh is, however, masked out with a stencil to form an envelope-shaped screen. You may either copy an attractive existing envelope, or follow the instructions for a standard-sized envelope below.

REQUIREMENTS
Stiff cardboard, 340 x 250 mm
Woòdglue or varnish as a sealer
Paintbrush

Draw the envelope shape on stiff card and cut along the pencil lines with a hobby knife. Leaving a margin of a few millimetres, remove the inside area and create an 'envelope stencil'. Seal the stencil with two coats of woodglue or varnish to prevent it from disintegrating after a few immersions in water.

To make the envelope, sandwich the stencil firmly between the mould and deckle and lift the pulp onto the mould as usual. After draining the mould for about 30 seconds, lift the deckle a fraction to allow the water lying on the stencil to drain off. Gently wiggle the envelope stencil with one hand to release the fibres overlapping its edges and lift it off the mesh. Be careful not to allow water to drip onto the mould and spoil the paper. Couch the envelope, following the same methods as for paper. Press and dry the envelopes and size them if you want to write on them with ink. Sizing will also strengthen them, which will be useful if you intend sending the envelopes by post. To fold them, simply fold in the side and bottom flaps and glue them down. Keep the original envelope or diagram as a guide to folding. Graph paper is also useful as a guide for accurate folding.

> **Note:** *Do not try to cut through thick card in one go. Firm pressure with the knife held at a 30-degree angle, and two or three cuts, will result in a cleaner edge. If your arms get tired, you are pressing too hard.*

The stencil can also be made of stiff plastic such as that used for overhead transparencies (sold at stationers) or X-rays. Plastic has the added advantage of being completely water-resistant.

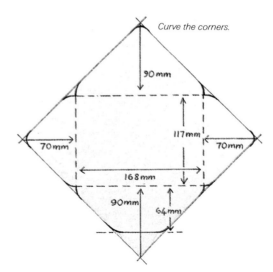

Curve the corners.

90 mm

117 mm

70 mm   70 mm

168 mm

90 mm   64 mm

Draw up the basic envelope shape.

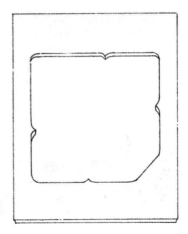

Cut the shape out of cardboard to form a stencil.

Seal the stencil with wood glue or varnish.

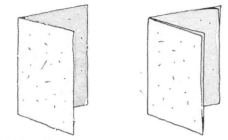

Fold A5 card in half or A4 paper into quarters.

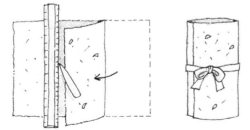

Fold paper into three and secure with ribbon.

Cards

There are three basic ways to make handmade paper cards that will fit in a standard-sized envelope:

1. Folding dry paper to the required size.
2. Tearing dry paper to the required size.
3. Forming thicker paper/card at the sheet-forming or couching stage.

Folding. An A5 sheet can be folded in half. The front can be plain or decorated with a simple design, and a message written inside.

An A4 sheet can be folded in four. Once it is folded twice, even thin paper will be strong enough to stand upright. After folding, mark the front and inside sections lightly with a pencil and open the folded sheet out flat. (Bear in mind that the lettering and design will be facing in opposite directions – while working on the one, the other will be upside down and diagonally opposite.)

Paper can also be folded in three across its width. Divide the paper into three (for an A4 sheet each panel will be about 100 mm wide), score along the fold-lines with a bone folder and fold the panels inwards so that they overlap.

> **Note:** When measuring paper for folding, take into account the total width of the paper, including any furry deckle edges. If you fold too tightly, these edges will be squashed.

Tearing. An A4 sheet of paper can also be torn in half to make two A5 sheets. Alternatively it can be torn in four to make smaller A6 cards, suitable for invitations. Bear in mind, however, that the paper needs to be thicker than that made in the projects so far. A disadvantage of tearing larger sheets to make smaller cards is that you lose the unique character of the soft deckle edge.

> **Note:** Never cut visible edges of handmade paper, as it destroys the effect. Tearing handmade paper is a useful skill that is invaluable when tearing any quality paper (such as Fabriano or Arches). First, firmly hold a ruler against the fold-line and score the paper with a bone folder or smooth, blunt knife. Then fold the paper along the scored crease and smooth the crease with a bone folder or back of a spoon. Fold the paper along the crease in the opposite direction and smooth it as before. The thicker the paper, the more folding will be necessary before tearing. To tear the paper, open it out and hold a ruler firmly against the fold with one hand. Grasp the opposite top corner of the page with the other hand and tear downwards slowly. The torn edge should resemble a deckle edge.
>
> Another method of tearing can be used in the case of thin paper such as Japanese paper or lightweight handmade paper. Simply mark the line you wish to tear with a thin pencil and lightly brush along it with a wet paintbrush. When the water has soaked through to the back of the paper, tear along the line. You will now have a soft rather than a hard edge. The advantage of this method is that it also enables you to tear on a curve.

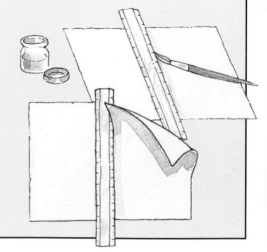

Making thicker paper or card while
couching. By increasing the amount of pulp in a vat, you will automatically form thicker sheets. Alternatively, couch two or three sheets of wet paper one on top of another (*see* Chapter 9 for laminating techniques). This is easier than it sounds, as each sheet of wet paper will naturally bond to the sheet below. The trick is to line up the mould accurately on top of the previously couched sheet and then to couch as usual.

Mountcards for photographs
Handmade paper cards form an attractive background for photographs. A novel idea for Christmas cards is to send family snapshots mounted on handmade cards. The handmade paper will need to be stiff enough to stand as a card and can be formed at the couching stage either by using thick pulp, or by laminating two or three sheets. When dry, fold the A4 (or A5) sheet in half, using a bone folder to score the fold, and position the photograph centrally on the front of the card. Mark the corners with a thin pencil line and

Mark off the position of the photograph with a pencil and cut diagonal slits in the card for inserting the corners of the photograph.

remove the photograph. Then mark a point on each line 10 mm from the corner and at each corner draw a diagonal line joining the two points. Carefully cut along these lines with a knife and insert the photograph by tucking the corners into the slits.

Thick paper cards make unique mounts for photographs.

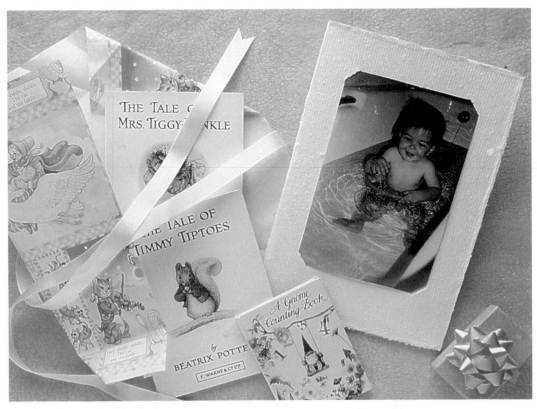

Art cards

Creative and colourful cards making the most of your artistic or design abilities can be created at the couching stage. Two methods will be outlined.

1. Squirting away the pulp

REQUIREMENTS
Garden hand-spray
A tub of thick pulp
A tub of thin pulp in a contrasting colour

Spraying away the pulp with a jet of water.

Using a mould and deckle, form a fairly thick base sheet in one colour and couch it onto wet felt. Wash away any pulp adhering to the mould and form a second sheet in a contrasting colour, using thinner pulp. Once the sheet has drained sufficiently, raise the mould to a vertical position and spray a fine jet of water from the nozzle of the garden spray bottle at it, either in random squiggles or controlled lines. This is best done outside, as the sprayed pulp will be plastered over your walls if you work inside. For added effect, spatter small 'watermarks' onto the mould, creating a textured surface on the paper. When you are happy with your pattern, couch it carefully on top of the first base sheet and cover it with another wet felt. Continue in this manner until you have made enough cards, press the pile of felts as usual and hang up to dry.

Art cards made by squirting away the pulp or by creating wet paper collages.

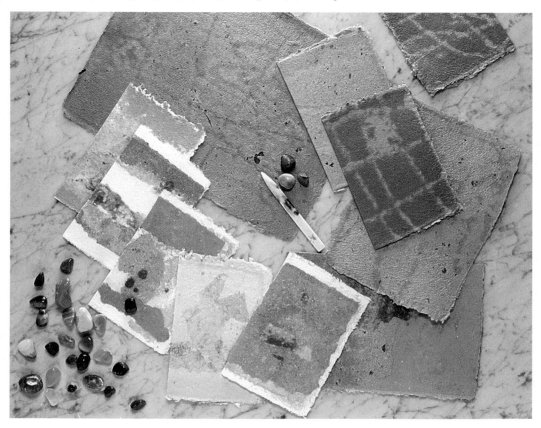

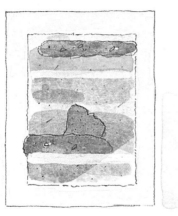

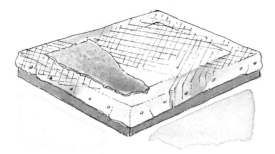

Position torn strips of paper onto the newly couched sheet. Dip a corner of the mould into thin pulp and couch it onto the collage.

2. Wet paper collages

REQUIREMENTS
Previously made handmade paper
A tub of thick pulp
One or two tubs of thin pulp in contrasting
colours

Using the thick pulp, form and couch a base sheet onto wet felt. On this wet sheet, place torn strips of handmade or tissue paper, and allow the moisture to seep through and dampen these strips. Then wash off the pulp adhering to the mould and dip an edge (or corner) of the mould into a tub of thin coloured pulp. Couch this somewhere on the base sheet and torn paper in such a way that the overlapping fibres of the pulp trap the torn paper. Continue in this way, layering the thin coloured pulp, until you are satisfied with the design. Lay a wet felt over the design and continue with the next one, until you have a post ready to press. Finally hang up the felts to dry.

Fold-cards

Handmade paper can be folded in unusual ways to highlight the attractive deckle edge. For example, insert a sheet of contrasting handmade or commercial paper, cut to size, in the folded paper for your message. The fold-card can be further enhanced by tying it with a satin ribbon or twisted gold thread. Unless you intend writing on them, these fold-cards need not be sized.

Rectangular fold-card

REQUIREMENTS
Sheet of handmade paper, A4 size
Contrasting paper, 100 x 160 mm

Copy the fold-lines in the diagram onto a plain piece of paper to act as a guide. Lay the A4 sheet of handmade paper over the plain paper and turn in the sides as indicated in the diagram.

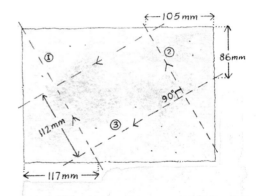

Diagram of fold-lines for rectangular fold-card.

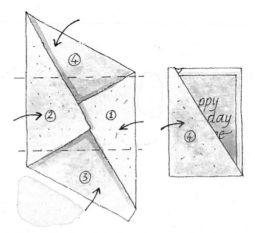

Fold the sides inwards in the order as numbered and insert a message card.

Square and round fold-cards.

Square fold-card

REQUIREMENTS
One sheet of handmade paper, 200 mm
*   square*
One sheet of handmade paper in a
*   contrasting colour, 180 mm square*
Commercial card
Satin ribbon or twisted thread,
*   500 mm long*

Form square sheets by making either a square
mould or square templates in the same way
as the envelope template. When dry, position
the smaller square centrally over the larger
one, using double-sided tape or folded
adhesive tape, and fold as indicated in the
diagram. Note where the fold-lines divide the
square in three. (The diagram can be enlarged
on a photocopier to the size you require, and
the fold-lines marked off on your paper with
a bone folder.) Inside the folded square, insert
a message on a piece of card. For added effect,
mark a coloured border round the edge of the
card with a felt-tipped pen.

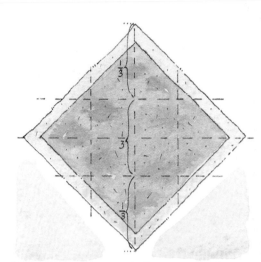

Position the smaller square in the centre of the larger
one and score fold-lines.

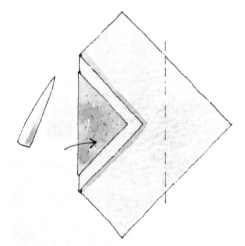

Fold sides towards the centre.

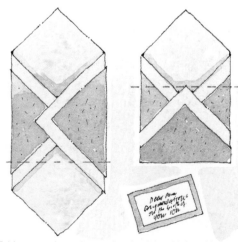

Fold corners inwards, overlapping by a third and insert a
message card.

Round fold-cards

There are two basic ways to make these cards:

Method 1

REQUIREMENTS
The same as for the square fold-card, but using two circular sheets in contrasting colours, one with a diameter about 20 mm less than the other

Round paper can be made on an embroidery frame with net curtaining stretched over it, or by using a circular template. Stick down the smaller circle in the centre of the larger one with double-sided tape and fold as indicated in the diagrams. Note that the edges are folded to the centre of the circle on all four sides. Insert the message card into the fold-card and tie a ribbon or twisted thread around it for a finishing touch.

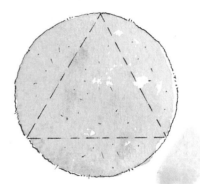

Draw an equilateral triangle inside the circle and fold the edges towards the centre.

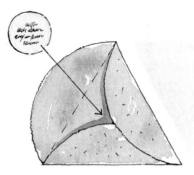

Insert a message card and tuck the last flap under the first.

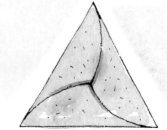

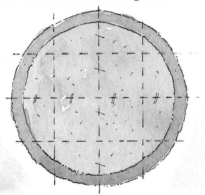

Position the smaller circle in the centre of the larger one and score fold-lines.

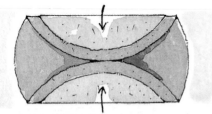

Fold the edges towards the centre.

Insert a message and tie the card with a ribbon.

Method 2

REQUIREMENTS
Compass
Round sheet of handmade paper
Commercial card

On a spare piece of paper, draw a circle the size of the handmade sheet. Set the compass at radius length and divide the circumference of the circle into six. Draw an equilateral triangle inside the circle (the sides of the triangle will also form the fold-lines). Using this as a guide, fold the sheet of handmade paper, smoothing the folds firmly with a bone folder. Insert a triangular or circular message card and tuck the flaps of the paper into one another as shown in the diagram.

Several sheets of paper can be joined in one long strip to make a zigzag Japanese fold-card.

Japanese fold-card

REQUIREMENTS
*Three to five sheets of A5 (or smaller)
  handmade paper*

This is an attractive way to use A5 (or smaller) sheets of paper. Fold the sheets of paper in half and overlap them by half the sheet, butting up to the fold. Make sure that all the edges line up when the card is folded before gluing. Press the folded card under weights for 24 hours. The card can be inserted into a standard-sized manila envelope as is, or can be threaded with a long ribbon. Punch holes in the card and pull the ribbon through, taking care not to tear the paper. Sized paper will be less likely to tear.

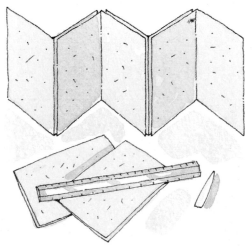

Overlap the folded sheets of paper by half each time, butting up to the fold.

Containers for gifts

Handmade paper makes an attractive wrapping for gifts, giving them a unique, personal touch.

Simple bags

REQUIREMENTS
Rectangular paper

Following the instructions in the diagram, first fold the sides of the paper towards the centre, with an overlap of 10 mm. Smooth the folds at the sides with a bone folder, glue down the overlap at the centre and press under weights for an hour. Then draw fold-lines 20 mm from both sides on the back and the front, and score with a bone folder. Fold towards the inside of the bag, pressing down well. Mark a fold-line 30 mm from the bottom and tear away the inner part of the flap as illustrated. Glue down the flap and press the bag under weights for 24 hours.

Pillow box

REQUIREMENTS
As for Simple bags

Draw the shape of the box on a spare piece of paper, marking fold-lines as dotted lines. Either use this as a guide for cutting and folding the handmade paper, or for making a template to use on a mould. Crease all fold-lines, fold the box in half on the centre fold-line and glue the flap under the opposite side. Place under weights for an hour. Then fold the top flaps inward to close the box. The box can be further enhanced by tying a satin ribbon around it.

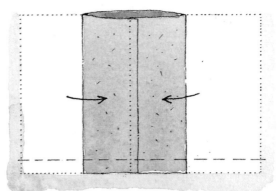

Fold both sides inwards to overlap at the centre.

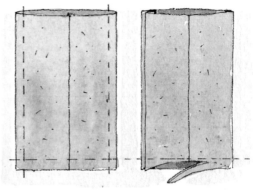

Tear away lower edge in a curve to reduce bulk.

Pillow box and gift bags.

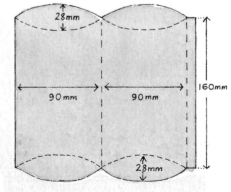

28mm

90 mm 90 mm 160mm

28mm

Diagram for pillow box.

Gift box

REQUIREMENTS
Thick cardboard
Two sheets of A4 handmade paper

You can cover existing boxes, or make your own according to the diagram. To make your own, mark out the base measurements of the box on a piece of cardboard, making sure that all lines are perpendicular to each other. Measure the sides of the box and add this measurement to that of the four sides of the base. Cut out the shape, fold along all scored lines and tape the corners together. To cover the box, mark out the basic box template on a sheet of handmade paper, allowing an extra 15 mm to the height of the sides for folding down inside the box. Add tuck-in flaps for glueing around the corners of the box. Apply glue to the handmade paper, working radially from the centre. Position the box centrally on the paper and press well. Glue the paper to the two shorter sides, folding over the top of

the box and smoothing the flaps around the corners. Then glue the remaining two sides. Press well with your fingers and turn the margin over the top edge. Follow the same procedure for a lid, but note that the lid will be slightly larger (about 2 mm all around) than the box, in order to fit over it. Measure carefully before cutting either the cardboard or the handmade paper.

Alternatively, cover an existing box with handmade paper. Simply open the box out flat and mark off the measurements of the base and sides on handmade paper, allowing an extra margin for tucking in at the top. On the two opposite shorter sides, draw 'tuck-in' flaps for folding under the longer sides at the corners. Cut out the covering paper and spread paste over it with a brush. Position the box carefully in the centre and glue down the shorter sides and 'tuck-ins' first, and then the longer sides. Finally, turn in the top margins. For a special gift box, you may first want to cover the inside of the box with marbled paper (*see* Chapter 9).

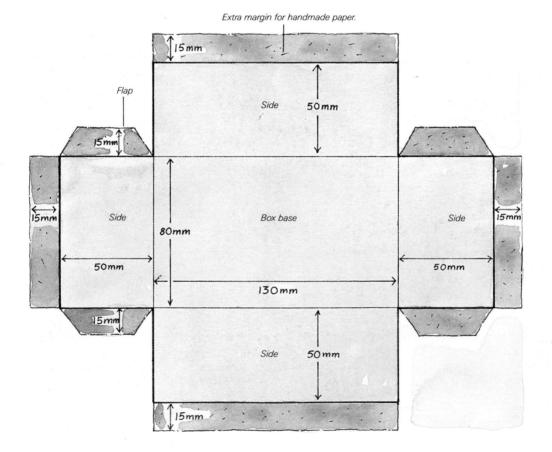

Extra margin for handmade paper.

15mm · Flap · 15mm · Side · 50mm · 15mm · Side · 80mm · Box base · Side · 15mm · 50mm · 50mm · 130mm · 15mm · Side · 50mm · 15mm

| Fold the eight threads in half and tie a knot 60 mm from the centre. | Tie every fourth thread to the embroidery frame. | Tie the remaining threads to the frame, spacing them evenly. | Tie the paper ovals in a spiral. |

Paper mobile

A colourful paper mobile can be an attractive addition to a child's room or a fun house-warming gift for a friend. Little scrolls of plant papers wrapped in silver thread, small animal shapes, colourful circles or squares can be hung from wire or an embroidery frame. The lightness of paper, and its exciting colour and texture combinations, can be an artistic accent as it moves gently in a breeze at an open window or doorway.

REQUIREMENTS
Embroidery frame, 200 mm in diameter
Crochet cotton
Darning needle
Paint
Clear matt varnish
Paintbrush
Turpentine
Thick pulps in a variety of colours
Wallpaper paste, mixed according to the
  instructions on the packet

Without using a frame, pour thick pulp onto dry felt in a roughly oval shape 80-100 mm long. Use as many colours as you have to make 16 such paper ovals. Lay another dry felt on top and mop carefully with a sponge until you have removed the excess water. Replace the now damp top felt with a dry one and roll gently with a rolling pin. Remove the

top felt and leave the paper ovals to dry on the base felt. When dry, place the ovals on newspaper and paint one side of each oval with wallpaper paste. When they are dry, paint the other side.

Meanwhile, paint the embroidery frame in a colour matching the ovals, applying two coats of paint, and then two coats of clear varnish. Remember to clean the brush with turpentine after use.

To assemble the mobile, first cut eight two-metre lengths of crochet cotton. Fold the bundle of threads in half and tie a knot in the centre, so that you have a 60 mm loop to hang on a hook. Hang the bundle of threads at a convenient height, ready for tying on the embroidery frame. Tie the 1st, 5th, 9th and 13th strands of cotton onto the frame about 300 mm away from the central knot, dividing the frame into four equal portions. Make sure that the frame hangs level: adjust the knots if necessary. Then tie on the other strands of thread, spacing them evenly round the frame. Decide on the colour order of your ovals, pierce a hole in the first one and tie it up so that it hangs about 120 mm from the frame. Repeat this procedure with the next oval, but tie it so that it hangs slightly lower than the first oval. Continue in this manner until you have created a spiral effect with your ovals. To complete the mobile, cut off all loose ends of cotton.

Chapter 9
Other paper craft techniques

Some of the crafts in this chapter require more specialised equipment and techniques. However, many exciting and original things can be done with handmade paper, leading you on to fascinating experiments with paper as an art form.

Handmade paper can be used as a mount for old photographs, either as a card as shown in Chapter 8, or within a frame. Laminating several sheets on top of one another creates thicker paper or card. This can be taken a step further, creating interesting surface textures by laminating objects between the sheets. Other raised surface designs can be created by means of embossing or embedding objects in the paper. Unsized paper is an excellent surface for printing on and printed handmade paper can, for example, make attractive cards, book covers, patterns for bags and boxes. Once you have accumulated a collection of beautiful handmade sheets, you can also bind them in a book.

Mounts for old photographs

Plant paper or onion-skin paper is particularly effective as a background for old family photographs.

REQUIREMENTS
Ready-made wooden frame
Wood stain (medium oak)
Wood sealer
Paintbrush, 10 mm wide
Gold poster paint
Very small paintbrush (No. 0)
Mounting-board

Sand the frame if necessary, stain it with wood stain and leave it to dry. You may want to apply more than one coat, depending on the shade you require. Cut the mounting-board to fit inside the frame, using a knife and steel ruler. Either position the sheet of handmade paper so that the deckle edge is visible (with a good margin all round), or cut it to fit the frame. Then cut the photograph to the size you require, position it centrally on the paper and mark the top corners with a thin pencil line as a guide for gluing down. For an attractive 'antique' finish, rule an edge of gold paint around the photograph with a paintbrush or gold felt-tipped pen.

Apply double-sided tape to the back of the photograph and position it carefully on the handmade paper, using the pencil marks as a guide. Press it under weights for 24 hours,

then assemble the frame, glass, mounting-board and handmade paper and fasten securely with pins or nails. Finally seal the back of the frame with strips of masking tape overlapping the mounting-board. For a professional finish, you could cover the back of the frame with brown paper.

Laminating and embossing

These two techniques involve working with newly formed wet sheets at the time of couching. Embossing works equally well with both the pouring and couching method of paper-making.

Laminating refers either to couching two or more sheets one on top of the other for extra thickness and to prevent cockling, or to sandwiching objects between the two sheets. For the best results, keep the pulp fairly thin. After couching one sheet onto a wet felt, position a flat object or objects on the wet sheet and couch a second sheet on top, sandwiching the object or objects between the two sheets. Anything from bits of wool, lace, string, feathers, ferns, pressed leaves and flowers, pine needles, torn tissue paper or cut-out letters could be placed between the sheets. For added interest paint the object(s) first – the paint will bleed through the paper, creating an interesting effect. Bear in mind that the colour of autumn leaves will run when sandwiched between two wet sheets of paper. It can look very beautiful, but if you want to eliminate this, boil and press the leaves first.

Embossing refers to a raised surface or relief design in paper, as is often used for company or personal logos, wedding invitations, etc. A sheet of damp paper, pressed onto a relief design, retains the image. You can use natural objects such as those listed under laminating for relief designs, or manufactured designs such as linocuts, cut-out letters, woven raffia or cane work.

First couch a sheet of paper onto thin fabric such as dressmakers' vilene or a man's handkerchief, and hang it up to dry for four to six hours to speed up the drying process. Then, while the paper is still slightly damp, lay an object such as a leaf, feather or fern on top of it. Cover it with another piece of dry fabric and iron the paper dry. The object will cause an impression on the paper.

Alternatively, you could allow the damp

paper to dry naturally on top of its relief object. Position the damp sheet of paper (still backed with its fabric) *over* the object on stiff board or card, and gently peel the fabric away. Lay a piece of foam (about 20 mm thick) over the damp paper and cover it with a board and weights for 24 hours. Remove the weights and board and carefully lift the foam to check. If the paper is still damp, cover it with a dry piece of foam (or possibly newspaper)

and press it again. Do not lift or remove the paper until it is bone-dry and the image pressed into it well.

Another embossing technique is to couch a sheet of paper directly onto a relief object such as a linocut. First prepare the linocut by spraying it with non-stick baking spray or rubbing the surface with talcum powder. Allow the wet sheets to dry completely before removing them.

String embossing with papyrus paper.

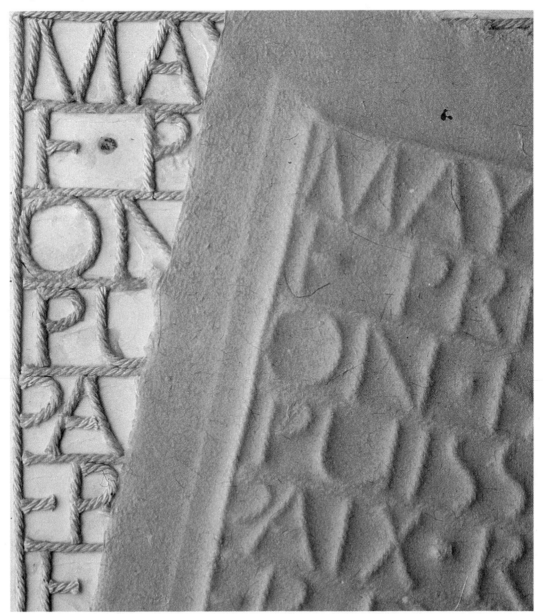

Simple printing on unsized paper

Printing techniques that work particularly well on unsized handmade paper are potato-cuts, linocuts and woodcuts.

Potato-cut printing

REQUIREMENTS
Potato
Container with a flat base (for example a plastic margarine tub)
Piece of thin sponge or foam rubber to fit in the tub
Powdered paint
Unsized paper

Lay out newspapers on a table as protection against the mess. Slice the potato in half cleanly, making sure that you have a smooth printing surface. Cut one half into a square shape. (At this point you can cut a handle to the potato to grip with.) Cut a few strips out of the potato in the design of your choice. Do not spend too much time worrying about a design – even the simplest or crudest of shapes can develop into the most exciting patterns when printed. Using a soft pencil, mark a light horizontal and vertical line on the unsized paper, slightly off-centre in each

Cut wedges out of the potato to create a design.

Cut a 'handle' on the potato.

Ink up the potato by pressing it onto the printing pad.

case. This acts as a guide for the first row of printing. Mix a little powdered paint with water in the plastic tub (try three heaped teaspoons of powder in a little water as a start), and press the sponge into it to soak up the paint. Turn over the sponge – this is your printing pad. Now press the cut surface of the potato block firmly onto the sponge and then onto the newspaper to see how it prints. Make adjustments to the block and to the density of the paint and do another test print. When you are satisfied with the thickness of the paint and the shape of the block, print your first row of potato prints, lining them up against one of the pencil lines. Either ink up the block with each printing or print two at a time. The second print will be slightly lighter in shade and can give an interesting texture to the pattern.

Linocutting

REQUIREMENTS
Linocutting or wood-cutting tools (available at hobby shops)
Lino
Oil-based ink
Roller
A piece of glass or a ceramic tile
Spoon

Draw a design on paper and transfer it to the lino by rubbing the back of the paper with a soft pencil or by slipping a piece of carbon between it and the lino, and retracing the lines with a pen. Mark in the areas you want to print and cut away the remainder. Before cutting, put the lino in the sun or in the airing cupboard to soften it – it will then be easier to cut. Be careful to cut away from you, otherwise you could cut yourself badly if the knife slips. For printing, first squeeze a teaspoonful of ink onto the surface of the glass (or tile) and spread it well with the roller. Then, using the roller, spread the ink over the lino until the raised surface is evenly inked up. Carefully lay the sheet of unsized, handmade paper over the block and press it down gently with the flat of your hand. Then rub the entire area with the back of a spoon to ensure that the whole surface of the lino makes good contact with the paper. To check whether the impression has taken, carefully lift a corner of the paper. When you are satisfied with the result, gently peel off the paper and lay it flat to dry.

Simple marbling

Marbling is the technique whereby a coloured pattern that resembles marble is transferred onto paper. It is associated mainly with bookbinding and the lining of gift boxes, but can also be used to create colourful notepaper and envelopes, folders or cards. Marbling relies on the fact that oil and water do not mix. Oil paints are floated on water and manipulated into a pattern. A sheet of paper is then laid on the surface and picks up the pattern. Usually commercial papers are used for this technique but handmade paper can be successfully marbled provided that it is well sized and has been allowed to 'stand' for a while. Such paper is particularly attractive as a background for hand-embroidery. The simplest method, using a minimum of equipment or expensive ingredients, is outlined below.

REQUIREMENTS
Shallow tray such as a cat litter tray or
  roasting pan
Oil paints in two colours
Turpentine
Two small jars for mixing colours
Two paintbrushes
Skewer or thin stick
Newspapers
Commercial or sized handmade paper

Fill the tray with cold water to a depth of about 80 mm. Keep some newspapers – laid out flat – close by. Squeeze about 20 mm of oil paint from each tube into a jar, one colour per jar. Add about 10 ml of turpentine to each colour and mix until the paint has the consistency of thin cream. Dip a paintbrush into the first colour and drop some paint onto the surface of the water to test its consistency. It should spread to about 20 mm in diameter. If the patch shrinks, the paint is too thick and needs to be thinned with more turpentine. If the patch spreads too wide and too fast, the paint is too thin and some more needs to be added.

When the consistency is right, drop paint randomly over the whole surface of the water by tapping the handle of the paintbrush against the side of the tray. Repeat with the second colour. To create a pattern, simply drag a skewer through the water in a slow zig-zag motion. Do not stir too much, or the paint will break up and become spotty. Lift your paper by grasping two diagonally opposite corners and lower it gently onto the surface of the water, smoothing out the sheet from the centre to the corners. Make certain that there are no trapped air bubbles, as these will create blank spots in your pattern. While smoothing out the bubbles, be sure not to submerge the paper.

Now lift out the paper carefully and lay it on the newspaper to dry, with the pattern side up. Between each printing, remove the excess paint from the surface of the water with rolled-up newspaper and repeat the process. When the marbled paper is dry, it can be pressed in a heavy book or under weights for a few days.

> **Note:** *An alternative method of marbling is to 'tie-dye' handmade paper. This is done by scrunching up the paper, tying it into a ball and immersing it in coloured dye for 2-4 hours. Allow the paper to dry thoroughly before carefully unwrapping the ball. When it is open, the process can be repeated with another colour, or the paper can be smoothed out and pressed under weights for a few days.*

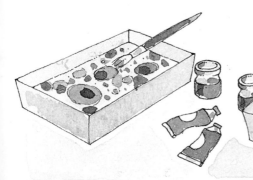

Drop paint onto the surface of the water.

Drag a skewer or pencil through the water to create a pattern.

Lower the paper onto the surface of the water.

Simple bookbinding

When you have accumulated a large quantity of handmade papers of varied texture and colour, you may wish to bind them in a beautiful leather binding. However, it is not necessary to bind it professionally to create an object of beauty. There are simple but very effective ways to bind books, even if you have no experience and only the minimum of equipment.

If you are a calligrapher, you could write quotes or poems in the books and turn them into treasured heirlooms.

REQUIREMENTS

Plain or patterned handmade or commercial
*   paper for the cover*
Buttonhole silk or crochet cotton (No. 8)
Thin darning needle
Six sheets of handmade paper
A pair of dividers

Fold the sheets of handmade paper in half and crease the fold firmly. Slip the pages inside one another to form a section. Mark out the measurements of the cover, allowing 3 mm outside the deckle edges at the head and tail, and 10 mm at the fore-edge. You will trim it later. Cut out the cover with a knife and steel ruler, then fold it in half and crease the fold with a bone folder. Slip the section inside the cover, leaving an equal margin at the top and bottom. Open out the book to the centre fold, find the centre point on the fold and mark it with a pencil. Measure 25 mm up from the tail and down from the head, and mark these points with a pencil. Check that the book still fits well into the cover and that the margins are still equal all round.

Using the darning needle, prick three holes through all layers of paper, including the cover. Cut a piece of thread 250 mm long, thread it through the needle and begin sewing through the middle hole in the centre of the book. Follow the diagram, sewing in a S-formation, until you push the needle through the centre hole again. Tie a knot in the thread and cut off the ends to about 10 mm. Close the book and mark a point on the inside cover at the fore-edge, allowing a 3-mm margin from the deckle edge. Use a pair of dividers (or strip of paper) to mark this measurement from the edge of the cover to act as a guide for cutting. Finally, cut the cover at the fore-edge with a knife and steel ruler. Press under weights for a week.

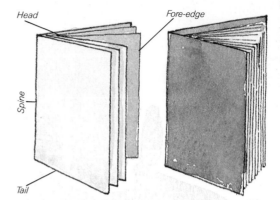

Slip the folded pages inside one another to form a section and slip the section inside the cover.

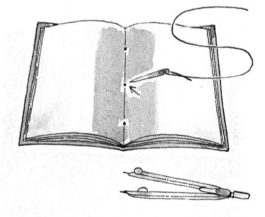

Prick three holes through the layers of paper and cover, and begin sewing through the middle hole.

Sew through the holes following the diagram.

Opposite: Simple bookbinding: single-section and Japanese fold-books. The cover at top of page is a paper-cast of a woodcut, done by Thelma Harwood.

From left to right: Japanese fold-book in Kozo fibre, concertina fold-book made from overlapping A4 sheets and miniature fold-book.

Japanese fold-book

A Japanese 'concertina' fold-book makes a lovely gift and is particularly charming when done as a miniature. It can be left blank for the recipient to write in, or could contain a poem or a short illustrated story for a child. The book can be made with one long strip of paper or by joining several sheets together. Below are the instructions for making a miniature out of one sheet of A4 handmade paper torn into three strips.

REQUIREMENTS
A sheet of handmade A4 paper
Wallpaper paste
Stiff cardboard for cover
Marbled commercial or handmade paper
  for cover
Greaseproof or wastepaper
Small paintbrush (about No. 2)

Mix the wallpaper paste by stirring 5 ml of powder into 250 ml of water. Let it stand for 24 hours. Stir occasionally. Then divide your A4 sheet lengthwise in three columns, each 70 mm wide, and mark the paper with a light pencil line at top and bottom. Lay a ruler against the pencil marks as a guide for the tear line, brush lightly with a wet paintbrush against the ruler and tear along the line. Repeat for the second tear. Now fold each strip carefully in four, smoothing the creases

with the bone folder as you go. To join the three strips, simply overlap a page at both ends of one strip with a page from each of the other strips and glue down firmly. Fold the paper so that it 'concertinas', with folds facing alternately front and back. When glued and folded, press under weights for 24 hours.

The cover is made from two identical pieces of cardboard, covered with decorative paper. To make the cover, draw up each cover on the cardboard with a pencil, allowing a margin of about 3 mm all round the fold-book. Include all deckle edges in your measurements. Check that the sides are squared and parallel and cut the cardboard with a knife. Make sure that both covers are identical and correct if necessary.

Now measure decorative paper for the cover, allowing an extra 10 mm wider than the card all round. Spread paste over the covering paper by brushing it radially from the centre. Remove the excess paper from the corners by cutting the paper diagonally approximately 3 mm away from the corner. Turn in the top and bottom flaps (head and tail) and press firmly against the card. Neatly tuck in the corner folds where they overlap the side flaps with a bone folder (see diagram). Then fold in the two side flaps, pressing well. Place a sheet of greaseproof paper on either side of the cover, and press under weights for 24 hours.

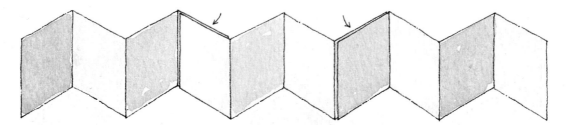

Join the strips by overlapping a page at each end.

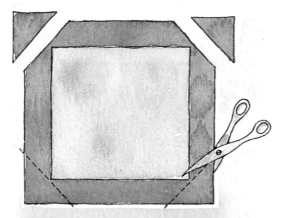

Remove excess paper 3 mm from the corner of the cover.

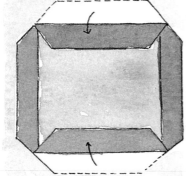

Turn the top and bottom flaps.

Tuck in the corner folds neatly against the card with a bone folder.

To assemble the book, open out the end pages of the folded book, keeping the two covers nearby. First paste up one end page and glue it to its cover, and then the other. Apply the paste carefully with a paintbrush, and make sure that no paste is brushed over the fold. Greaseproof paper laid over the adjoining page may help. Attach the pasted end page centrally onto the cover, smoothing it down well. Place greaseproof paper over the end page and rub down firmly with a bone folder. Leave the greaseproof paper where it is and paste up the other cover. Be especially careful to line up the two covers so that they match exactly before gluing the second cover. When both covers are attached to the book, place fresh greaseproof paper between the covers and adjacent pages of the book and press under weights for two to three days.

Ribbons glued between the covers and end pages make an attractive addition to the cover. Cut two ribbons 400 mm long and glue them centrally on the two inside covers before pasting these on the end pages.

Glue ribbons to the cover before attaching the end pages.

Glue end pages to each cover.

Chapter 10
Paper art

Many people imagine that 'paper art' techniques involve origami, paper cut-outs, paper collages, puppets, stage sets or papier-mâché. However, while paper art is none of these things specifically, it can include several elements of each of them.

As in the case of origami, paper cut-outs or collages, dry paper can be folded, cut, torn, punctured, sewn, woven, embossed and painted to form assemblages and collages with unusual tactile depth and richness. Damp paper can be laid over sculpted forms in a way that resembles puppet-making. Large assemblages and constructions may have the flavour of stage set design. However, papier-mâché bears the closest resemblance to much of what is understood as paper art, for it involves working with the basic paper pulp itself.

Wet paper pulp has a unique flexibility and three-dimensional quality different from any other art medium. Wet pulp resembles sloppy bread dough, filling in spaces and faithfully reproducing the shape and texture of the surface against which it dries. One can embed objects in it, or it can be cast into moulds or poured thickly in abstract designs with exciting colours and textures. Thick, drained pulp can be easily manipulated by pressing shapes into it, or heaping it so as to create raised surfaces. It can also be modelled and shaped in a fairly controlled fashion, similar to clay. This quality lends itself to an art form known as paper sculpture.

In addition, by using the couching method, thin translucent sheets of tinted paper can be layered to create depth and subtle colour combinations, sometimes revealing laminated objects underneath the surface. Partially dried paper can be overlapped, folded or twisted, creating interesting relief patterns of light and shade. In combination with other media, such as embroidery, weaving, lettering, pastels, pottery and sculpture, paper is beginning to capture the attention of artists in both the East and West.

Paper art techniques can be time-consuming, often requiring long drying periods or elaborate equipment or constructions. This chapter aims to give you an idea of some of the possibilities of the medium, using simple equipment. None of these projects takes up too much time. Once you have tried some of these techniques your imagination is sure to stimulate further experimentation of your own.

The 'R' is taken from a plaster cast of lettering done in sand. The alphabet is cast from a woodcut by Martin Field.

Paper-casting

Thick paper pulp can be poured over a variety of textured and relief surfaces to create intriguing paper-casts.

REQUIREMENTS
A bucket of pulp (plain white or tinted)
Frame or strips of wood
Two pieces of felt or fabric
Jug
Rolling pin
Absorbent sponge
Interesting surfaces or objects
Net bag or sieve
Non-stick baking spray

Drain the pulp through a net bag or sieve until it is quite thick, but still runny enough to be poured. Choose an interesting surface onto which to pour the pulp, such as a door mat, tree trunk, pile of stones or shells, patterned beach sand, tractor tyre, flotsam and jetsam picked up on the beach, wood carving, linocut or sculpture, or create your own surface. To make your own moulded surface, place objects such as twisted rope, folded fabric, pottery chips, seed pods or stones on a wooden board. Spray all surfaces that will be in contact with the pulp with non-stick baking spray. Position a wooden frame around the objects and pour a thick layer of pulp into it. Spread the layer evenly with your fingers and make sure that all raised areas are covered.

Place a piece of felt or fabric over the pulp and press down gently. Mop up the excess water seeping through the fabric with a sponge until the pulp is compressed and firm. At this point reinforce any thin, weak areas with more pulp. Gently remove the frame and replace the wet felt with a dry one. Press the dry felt down gently to absorb more water, then press more firmly with a rolling pin. Remove the felt and place the paper cast in the sun to dry. Depending on the weather and size of the mould, this should take between one and three days.

Make your own casting mould

There are several ways of making your own casting mould, using plasticine, plaster of Paris, rubber latex, or cardboard cut-outs.

❑ Plasticine is excellent for creating a simple casting mould. When making intricate designs, however, the plasticine tends to come away with the pulp when you remove the cast. Warm the plasticine in the sun or airing cupboard for 15-30 minutes to soften it, and then roll it out flat on a board with a rolling pin. Press objects such as nails, forks, corks, scone cutters, wrought iron, bent wire or beads into the plasticine. This can be quite random, as the effects created when pouring plain or coloured pulp into a three-dimensional mould can be surprisingly effective, even if the indentations in the plasticine are made quite casually.

You may leave the randomly shaped plasticine as it is, or cut it into a square or rectangular shape with a sharp knife. You can then pour directly onto the mould (creating an irregular edge), or make a frame around your 'casting mould' to contain the pulp. Simply cut a 30-mm strip of cardboard long enough to make a frame around the plasticine, and glue or tape the two ends together. Pour pulp into the mould as above and place it in the sun to dry.

❑ Plaster of Paris will form a more solid and permanent mould, suitable for several castings. Mix the plaster of Paris in the ratio of 1 part plaster of Paris to 1 part water, adding the dry powder slowly to the water. The plaster can be poured over interesting objects or patterned beach sand to create a mould. You can create face masks by applying dampened surgical bandage to a greased face and spreading a layer of plaster of Paris over it. When it is dry, remove the mask, spread a second layer of plaster of Paris over it and leave to harden. Press paper pulp into this cast and leave to dry. For large moulds, the plaster can be reinforced with fabric such as hessian or burlap.

❑ Cardboard cut-outs pasted on thick cardboard or wood are an inexpensive way to create a simple relief surface for casting paper pulp or 'laminate casting'. Corrugated cardboard also gives an interesting ribbed effect to the surface.

Plaster of Paris is poured onto sand and objects inside the frame.

Embedding objects in thick pulp

The opposite technique to the above is to pour thick pulp into an area defined by a frame and then press objects onto it. Then pour a little more pulp over to secure them. When the paper is dry, the fibres will cling to the objects, holding them in place. Moreover, some of the objects can be removed, leaving their shape embedded in the dry paper. Some objects can first be painted, or metal objects used. The latter will rust when in contact with the wet pulp and the rust stains will bleed interestingly into the wet pulp.

Pouring thick coloured pulp onto a screen or board

Thick coloured pulp can be poured onto a screen or board to form exciting variations in colour and texture. When using a screen, the interest lies in the contrast between the texture of the upper surface and that created by the mesh, whereas in the case of the board, one sees the smooth flat surface created by the board.

1. Pouring thick pulp onto a silk screen or mould

REQUIREMENTS
A bucket of pulp, drained until very thick
Colouring agents
Yoghurt cartons
Spoons for mixing colours
Mould or silk screen

Mix your colours in yoghurt cartons using a little water, add 500 ml of drained pulp to each carton and stir well. Bear in mind that the wet colour will be at least twice as intense as when the paper is dry. Leave the newly mixed colours to stand for at least two hours, as this helps prevent them from bleeding into each other on the screen.

Plan a design of coloured bands or curves and begin pouring thick pulp over the screen. You can dispense with a frame to contain the pulp if you prefer a random edge. Make sure that the edges of the different colours mesh well, or you will have holes in your paper. To create straight edges, use strips of wood as containments for the pulp.

When your design is finished, remove excess water from the screen by carefully mopping the underside of the mesh with a sponge, and then lay the screen flat in the sun to dry. After a few hours it will be safe to tilt the screen onto its side. Depending on the weather, it should take 1-3 days to dry. Once dry, the piece can be further worked on by dripping thick pulp onto it or embedding fabric, wool, shells, seed pods and other oddments in it. When the piece is finished to your satisfaction, remove it from the screen by working round the edge with a knife.

A variation on the above method is to first pour thin white pulp over the entire screen as a foundation layer. When this layer is dry, you can pour the different colours of your design. This will strengthen the sheet and eliminate the problem of holes or thin areas appearing once the paper is dry.

> **Note:** *Another method of strengthening your sheet is to add premixed wallpaper paste to the pulp before pouring it onto the foundation layer on the screen. Wallpaper paste has the added advantage of preventing bacterial action in your pulp and discouraging attacks by insects. Add one cupful of premixed wallpaper paste to a bucket of drained pulp.*

2. Pouring thick pulp onto a board

REQUIREMENTS
As above, but use a board instead of a mould or screen
Piece of thin fabric or large felt

The advantage of this method is that you can draw a design on the board as a guide to applying the pulp. Furthermore the flat surface created by pouring onto smooth board can later be sized and used to write on. Follow the instructions for the screen method, but mop up excess water with a sponge *outside* the area of wet pulp as it is applied. When the entire design is complete, lay a piece of fabric over it and use a sponge to mop up the moisture seeping through the fabric. Once most of the excess water has been removed, lay the board flat in the sun to dry until it can safely be tilted onto its side without the pulp sliding off. When dry, slide a long knife between the paper and board and work it slowly and carefully under the paper until it lifts off cleanly.

> **Warning:** *For this method, do not add wallpaper paste to the pulp, or it will not come off the board.*

The translucent layers of the 'patchworking' method.

Paper collages

'Patchworking'

With this technique you use a mould to form sheets of paper and couch several overlapping sheets to make a bigger one: the edges overlap, bonding the paper together. This can form a base for some of the other techniques and can be particularly attractive if several different colours are used.

REQUIREMENTS
Large piece of finely woven fabric, such as a
*   bedsheet or tablecloth*
Colouring agents
A5 or A4 mould
Bucket of plain pulp
Absorbent sponge
Four baby baths or washing-up bowls

First mix three colours of thick pulp in yoghurt cartons and leave them to stand for two hours. Then prepare a tub of water containing 2 ℓ of plain pulp, ready for forming sheets of paper. Wet the fabric thoroughly and stretch it out flat and straight onto a smooth surface, for example a kitchen table. Make sure that there are no air bubbles underneath. Form a sheet of paper with plain pulp, position the mould upside down somewhere on the fabric and use a sponge to mop up the excess water at the back of the screen (the side that is now uppermost). When it is no longer wet, lift one side of the mould gently to test whether it will come away, leaving the sheet on the fabric. If not, mop once more.

Make another sheet of paper and couch it next to the first in the same manner, overlapping an edge slightly. Mop as before. Continue in this way, overlapping the sheets to create a large sheet of paper in any shape or size you wish. Your only limit is the size of your fabric.

To apply overlapping coloured layers, you will first need to dilute the coloured pulp and stir it well to disperse the fibres. Pour a small quantity of the diluted coloured pulp into the spare tubs and make thin coloured sheets. For unusually shaped layers, either form whole sheets or merely dip an edge or corner of the mould into the pulp. Build up layers of overlapping thin, translucent sheets in different colours until you have created an interesting sheet of paper. This can form a colourful background for calligraphy or embroidery, or be made into a screen.

Making a screen

The overlap method for making large sheets of paper can be expanded to create interesting screens. Simply leave the paper on the fabric and size well, using one of the methods mentioned in Chapter 5. When the screen is dry, turn in a neat hem and nail or tack the fabric onto a wooden framework. If the paper has dried unevenly, size the paper and fabric again and gently stretch it to fit the frame. At this point, additional colours could be squirted or painted onto the paper to improve the design, or additional pieces of paper or fabric can be hand-embroidered onto it.

> *Note: The overlap technique can also be applied directly to a board. The advantage is that it will dry flat. It can then form a base for sculptural effects like twisted damp sheets (see p 86).*

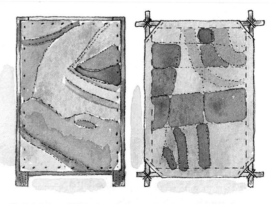

Tack fabric with its sheet of paper onto a wooden frame or sew a wide margin and thread bamboo sticks through all four sides.

Sculptural collages

Sculptural effects, by means of folding, twisting or scrunching damp sheets and applying them to a preformed wet sheet, can give a new dimension to the paper. Sculptural forms with contrasting textures can be added to paper either couched directly onto a board, or to wet paper left on the mould.

REQUIREMENTS
1½ ℓ of prepared pulp
Thin dishcloths or pieces of dressmakers' vilene cut larger than your mould
Deckle-box and mould
Absorbent sponge

Using the deckle-box, make one or two sheets of paper, couch onto dishcloths or vilene and hang up to dry in the sun for about an hour, or indoors for 3-5 hours. In the meantime, form another sheet of paper using the deckle-box. Leave it on the screen or couch it onto a board. Then, when the paper on the vilene is still damp, but dry enough to be removed, slip a knife under one corner and peel the fabric away slightly. If the paper handles easily and is not too soggy and floppy, it is ready. If not, leave it to dry for a

little longer. Keep the preformed sheet on the mould or board nearby.

Remove the damp sheets from the fabric, one at a time, and fold or twist them into interesting shapes. Position them on the paper on the mould, applying a little pressure to make them stick. The preformed sheet on the mould should not be too dry for the sculpted sheets to stick successfully. For added interest, bits and pieces of previously made paper or interesting fabric can be soaked briefly and wedged in amongst the folds. Leave the mould to dry naturally, lying flat and away from strong heat. When the whole assemblage is dry, remove it carefully with a knife.

Constructions

By draping paper over sticks, bamboo or cane, you can create elaborate three-dimensional 'sculptures' that invite the eye to look beyond and behind the surface. This is particularly beautiful when working with thin, translucent plant papers. The addition of beads, bones, shells, oddments of rolled paper, wool and fabric hung from the framework can turn the construction into a fascinating wall-hanging or mural.

Damp paper can be twisted and folded and attached to a wet sheet still on the mould.

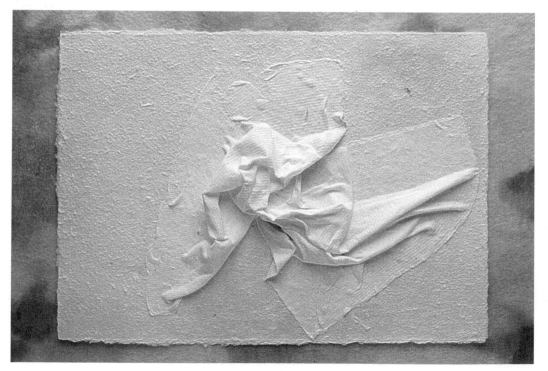

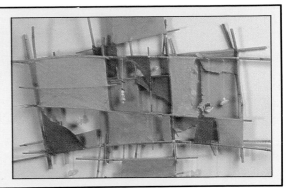

Note: *An alternative way of draping paper over sticks is to tear and drape the paper while it is still damp. In this way it will shrink round the sticks as it dries. This is very effective when thin translucent plant papers are draped over a curved surface. When dry, it looks very good with a light shining behind it. Simply couch the paper directly onto a board, lift the entire sheet or part of it, and drape it over the construction. It helps to paint the sticks with wallpaper paste prior to draping to ensure a good strong bond.*

Draping paper over a stick or bamboo construction.

REQUIREMENTS
Dry preformed handmade paper
Sticks, bamboo or reed stems
Beige crochet cotton
Scissors
Premixed wallpaper paste
Paintbrush

Tie together the construction – either on one flat plane, or several layers of separate constructions. Lay a sheet of paper against a corner you wish to drape and mark off a tear line with a wet paintbrush. Allow a sufficient margin for folding round the sticks. Tear the paper and apply wallpaper paste to the edge of the paper and to the sticks that it will be in contact with. Drape the paper over the sticks immediately and fold it over. To ensure good contact, smooth over the contact points with the paintbrush. Continue in this manner, carefully planning where you want paper and where you want gaps. This is particularly important if you are working with several layers of constructions. When you are satisfied with the effect, you may want to add beads, shells, rolls of paper or other oddments for interest.

Bowls

Paper bowls are very satisfying to make, whether left plain, or painted with a design. Many overseas artists incorporate sticks, beads, embroidery, masks and other sculptural effects in their bowls, turning them into works of art in their own right. There are two ways of casting bowls. The first is to apply thick paper pulp to the inner or outer surface of an existing bowl. The pulp may contain premixed wallpaper paste and the bowl is greased or lined with cling wrap prior to application of the pulp.

The second method, termed 'laminate casting', uses preformed sheets of paper couched directly onto a board. Tear off small pieces of this paper while it is still damp and apply them to the greased bowl, overlapping the torn feathery edges. After two or three layers of these overlapping pieces have been applied, the bowl is left to dry. The bowl is then sprayed with methyl cellulose or painted with a dilute solution of wallpaper paste. Depending on the thickness required, a further two or three layers of overlapping

Torn pieces of damp, freshly formed paper, applied to a smooth, greased surface.

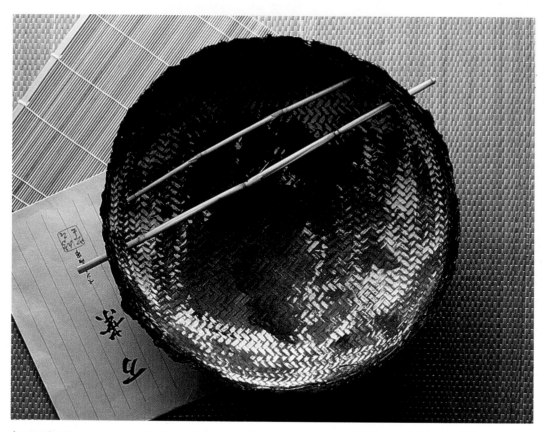

A paper bowl made by laminating small pieces of freshly formed paper onto a woven basket.

paper strips may be applied. The bowl is dried again and then sealed well with wallpaper paste. Bear in mind that if you want to paint the bowl, this must be done before the paste is applied, or the paint will not spread well.

It is possible to apply both of these methods to any curved surface, such as woven baskets, balls, balloons, colanders, casserole dishes or plates. Remember to grease or line the surface that will be covered with the paper and not to remove the paper cast until it is dry. To remove, simply slide a blunt knife between the bowl and the cast and work it around the whole bowl until the vacuum is broken. Lift the cast off the bowl and paint or seal the inside with wallpaper paste for strength.

Papier-mâché

A book on paper arts and crafts would not be complete without mentioning papier-mâché. The art of making objects from papier-mâché has existed about as long as paper-making and probably also originated with the Chinese, who used papier-mâché to create images used in religious festivals. In Europe it gained popularity in the Victorian period, when it was used to make decorative and resilient household articles such as boxes, trays, shelves and furniture. These were finished with several layers of paint and glossy lacquers.

The term papier-mâché originally meant 'made of pulped paper' or literally 'chewed paper', which is now termed mash. Nowadays, it has come to include making paper objects by pasting several layers of torn paper strips onto a mould until the required strength and thickness is achieved.

Today, many articles are still made of papier-mâché: folders, dolls, stage masks and props, and scenery for electric train sets, amongst others. Artists have re-acquainted themselves with papier-mâché as a sculpting medium, often in combination with painting, acrylics, embroidery and other popular handcrafts.

This section will mainly cover papier-mâché in its original sense, as 'pulped paper', with a brief outline of the more commonly known method, that of pasting torn strips of paper onto a mould.

Papier-mâché using torn strips

Any kind of paper suitable for making paper pulp will also be suitable for papier-mâché. The paper should be torn and not cut, as torn paper has softer edges, making the overlaps less obvious. Many books on papier-mâché suggest using newspaper, but because of the method of processing the fibres, newspaper is sometimes prone to acid attack and is best avoided for long-lasting articles. The object you use for a mould should be smooth-sided, such as a bowl, plate or ball.

REQUIREMENTS
Torn paper strips
Premixed wallpaper paste
Shallow bowl
Smooth object for a mould
Vaseline

Tear several sheets of paper into small strips and soak these in water. Spread Vaseline over the surface of the mould, or spray it with non-stick baking spray. Build up a layer of paper on the mould, overlapping the strips. The first layer is applied without paste, to prevent the paper from sticking to the mould when dry. When the first layer is complete, paint it with wallpaper paste. Then apply the second layer, painting the inside surface of each strip prior to applying it to the previous layer. You could use different colours for the successive layers, as this makes it easy to see whether the whole area has been covered. Paste three or four layers of paper and then place the object in a warm place to dry.

When dry, paste on another three or four layers, until the desired thickness is reached. Leave to dry in a warm place for a few days. To release your papier-mâché object, slide a blunt knife between the paper and the mould and work it around the edge until it comes free. Don't try to hurry this step or you could tear the papier-mâché. To finish the object, you can give it a fine sandpapering to remove rough edges. Seal the object by painting it with wallpaper paste. An attractive alternative is to give it two coats of paint (artists' gouache, oil paints, acrylics or PVA), followed by a coat of clear matt varnish.

Mash

This method is particularly suited to modelling face masks or pressing into plaster of Paris moulds. It has even been used to make furniture. Mash usually needs a basic supporting structure such as modelled clay or carved polystyrene. Supporting moulds can also be made from crumpled tinfoil or bent chicken wire. A first layer of torn paper strips laid over the wire or foil acts as a foundation for the mash. Mash can also be applied to a permanent construction, such as the skeleton of a chair, bowl, doll etc., the foundation remaining inside or under the layer of mash.

REQUIREMENTS
One bucket of prepared pulp
Net bag or nylon stocking
Premixed wallpaper paste
Mould
Vaseline

Drain the bucket of pulp through a stocking or net bag, squeezing until it is almost dry. Add one cup of wallpaper paste and boil the pulp and paste until it is tacky and smooth and the water content is reduced. This makes the mash stiffer and easier to model. Grease the surface to be modelled (if you intend to remove it from the cast when the mash is dry) and then spread the mash over it, pressing firmly with your hands. As dried mash tends to have a slightly lumpy appearance, 'buttering' it with a spatula or pressing it with a spoon will result in a smoother surface. However, because of the rough texture of dried mash, you may prefer to create a reverse mould into which to press the mash. A plaster of Paris casting of the object, such as a face mask, works well.

> **Note:** *While papier-mâché resembles the previously outlined techniques such as laminate and paper-casting, there are subtle differences. In the case of papier-mâché the mash is created by boiling up thick pulp with paste until it is stiff and tacky, while the casting techniques described above use pulp that is simply drained. The addition of paste is optional. Laminate casting uses torn strips of freshly formed paper, relying on the bonding properties of the cellulose in the fibres to glue the strips together, while papier-mâché uses dry, ready-made paper strips to which paste is applied.*

Other people's work

An increasing number of artists today are experimenting with paper as an art medium, either on its own or with other media. While several contemporary artists have been exploring the three-dimensional quality of paper in their art, it is beyond the scope of this book to represent them all. However, this section shows a few striking examples of the versatility and flexibility of paper by a few talented artists who specialise in a particular aspect of paper art.

Karlien de Haas (age 6)   *The rainbow*   310 x 220 mm
Karlien designed this work and chose the colours herself. The idea behind the piece was a landscape which included a rainbow. She began with the rainbow, pouring thin pulp onto an A4 mould and the flowers and landscape were added later in thicker pulp. Bright flowers were crayoned in as a finishing touch. As Karlien is left-handed, her signature reads from right to left, rather than the other way around.

Heleen de Haas   *Broken diagonal*   630 x 480 mm
Heleen works with thick pulp in bright colours, pouring them onto a large silkscreen. She enjoys working with the tactile dimension of the pulp and describes her work as being a combination of painting and sculpture — the pulp can either be fairly fluid and applied like a wash, or used very thick and manipulated like clay. This method is described on page 84.

Heleen de Haas
Heleen's method of working, pouring the pulp directly onto the upper surface of a fine-gauge silkscreen is clearly shown on the right.

Rose Denovan *Bay of tranquillity* 560 x 680 mm
Rose worked with several bowls of coloured pulp, built up on a grooved board to make this piece. Once dry, the paper was removed and worked further. The cliffs were drawn with oil crayon while the white waves were painted with gouache.

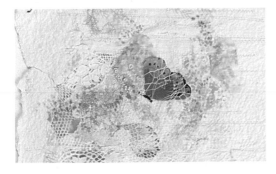

Rose Denovan *Seen through lace curtains*
The detail above includes both paper-making and embroidery. The paper was poured onto a board and backed with fabric for strength. Once dry the piece was embroidered by hand and machine.

Lin Kerr *How can one buy or sell the air* 500 x 400 mm
Lin is both a paper-maker and calligrapher and these skills are used to best advantage in this striking piece. She used natural materials such as palm fibres, wool and cotton thread, and gelatine sizing, to create a 'woven carpet' look in earthy colours.

Further reading

Paper-making

Barrett, T. *Japanese Papermaking – Traditions, Tools and Techniques*, Weatherhill, New York and Tokyo, 1983.

Bell, Lilian A. *Plant Fibers for Papermaking*, Liliaceae Press, McMinnville, Oregon, 1988.

Heller, J. *Paper-making*, Watson-Guptill, New York, 1978.

Hughes, S. *Washi, the World of Japanese Paper*, Kodansha International, Tokyo, 1978.

Hunter, D. *Papermaking: The History and Technique of an Ancient Craft*, Dover Publications, New York, 1978.

Richardson, M. *Plant Papers*, Berrington Press, Hereford, 1986.

Stearns, Lynn. *Papermaking for Basketry*, Press de LaPlantz, Inc., Bayside, California, 1988.

Studley, V. *The Art and Craft of Handmade Paper*, Studio Vista, London, 1987.

Toale, Bernard. *The Art of Papermaking*, Davis Publications, Inc., Worcester, Massachusetts, 1983.

Paper and other related crafts

Ashman, J. *Bookbinding, A Beginner's Manual*, A & C Black Ltd., London, 1981.

Banister, M. *Bookbinding as a Handcraft*, Sterling Publishers Inc., New York, 1975.

Bussi, Cathy. *Pressed Flowers, A Creative Guide*, New Holland (Publishers), London, 1988.

Chambers, Anne. *A Practical Guide to Marbling Paper*, Thames & Hudson, London, 1986.

Green, P. *Introducing Surface Printing*, Batsford Ltd., London, 1967.

Kenny C. and J. *Design in Papier-Mâché*, Pitman & Sons, London, 1973.

Maile, Anne. *Tie-dyed Paper*, Mills & Boon Ltd., London, 1975.

Pretorius, Anika. *Gifts from the Home, A Creative Book of Ideas for Giving*, New Holland (Publishers), London, 1989.

Shannon, Faith. *Paper Pleasures*, Mitchell Beazley, London, 1987.

Strose, S. *Potato Printing*, Sterling, New York, 1968.

Useful addresses

Dryad Craft Centre
Hand Paper-making Equipment
178 Kensington High Street
London W8 7RG
England

Falkiner Fine Papers Ltd
Fine Handmade Papers
76 Southampton Row
London WC1B 4AR
England

Wookey Hole Caves and Papermill
Handmade Papers
New Wells
Somerset
England

Lee S. McDonald Inc.
Fine Hand Paper-making Equipment
P.O. Box 264
Charlestown, MA 02129
USA

Twinrocker
Handmade Paper and Paper-making Supplies
P.O. Box 413
Brookston, IN 47923
USA

Hand Papermaking (Journal)
P.O. Box 10571
Minneapolis, MN 55458
USA

Index

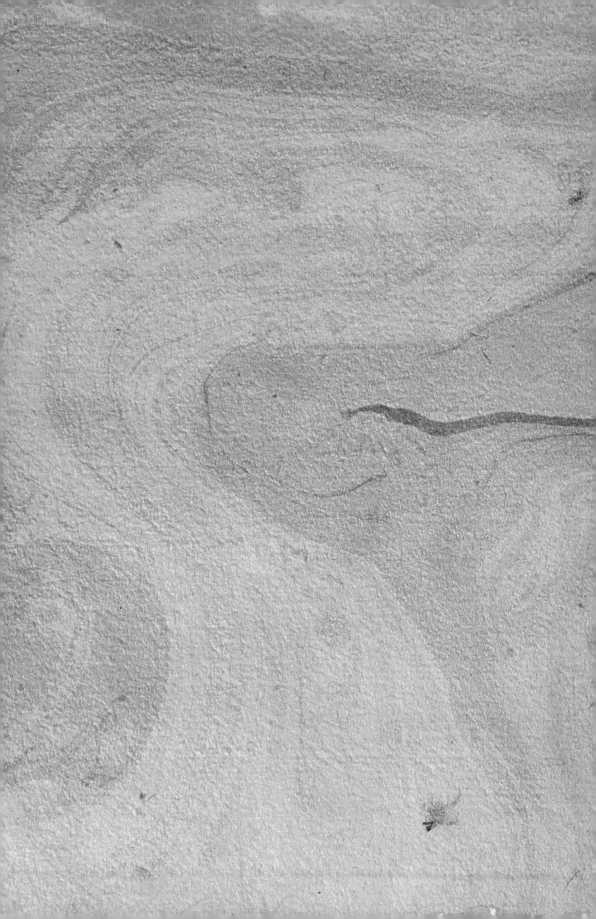

LAWRENCE DALLAGLIO

My Italian Family COOKBOOK

recipes from three generations

SIMON &
SCHUSTER
ILLUSTRATED

London · New York · Sydney · Toronto

A CBS COMPANY

LAWRENCE DALLAGLIO

My Italian Family
COOKBOOK
recipes from three generations

To Vincenzo, Alice, Ella, Josie and Enzo,
not forgetting my dear sister Francesca
and my mother Eileen, who have all been,
and continue to be, my inspiration.

Powerful together.

First published in Great Britain
by Simon & Schuster UK Ltd, 2011
A CBS COMPANY

1 3 5 7 9 10 8 6 4 2

SIMON & SCHUSTER
ILLUSTRATED BOOKS
Simon & Schuster UK Ltd
222 Gray's Inn Road
London
WC1X 8HB

www.simonandschuster.co.uk

Simon & Schuster Australia
Sydney

A CIP catalogue record for this book is available from the British Library

ISBN 978-0-85720-271-0
ISBN 978-0-85720-562-9 (corporate edition)

Editorial director: Francine Lawrence
Project editor: Hilary Ivory
Design: XAB Design
Photography: Ruth Jenkinson and Steve Baxter
Home economy: Emma Marsden
Production manager: Katherine Thornton
Commercial director: Ami Richards

Colour reproduction by Dot Gradations Ltd, UK
Printed and bound in China

My Italian Family COOKBOOK

what my father taught me...

I've been passionate about food from as far back as I can remember. Not just eating it, but all the sensory rituals that go with it: tracking down the best ingredients; the chopping, stirring, sizzling, hissing; the aroma of Bolognese bubbling on the hob. Smell can, in an instant, send me hurtling back in time to warm summer holidays spent in my grandmother's kitchen in Italy.

My dad, Vincenzo, a native of Turin and the embodiment of all things Italian – fine food, good wine and Juventus – spent a lifetime in the food business. Starting off at the Lido in Venice, he climbed the ladder via top-class hotels across the world before arriving at the London Metropole. Am I the only boy who, at age 12, enjoyed a six-month stay in the Westminster Suite at the top of the Metropole? My parents were house-hunting at the time and, looking back on it, this was probably where my love of good food started. There can't have been many youngsters in England who breakfasted on smoked salmon and scrambled eggs, then went to school with croissants for the boys at break. If that was kick-off most mornings, close of play was equally impressive, usually spent in the grill room dining on lemon sole or sea bass. It was a hell of a way for a boy to educate his palate.

Just as unusually for that era, when he wasn't tied up at work Dad did a lot of the cooking. Nowadays I tell Enzo, my 10-year-old, that if he can't cook he needn't expect to achieve babe-magnet status – it's definitely a skill that adds a certain something to a guy's social life. In fact, being able to cook was one of the few things that impressed Alice, now my wife! At his age, I vividly remember the admiration of friends who would drop by and, as always in our house, chat at the kitchen table while my father prepared a meal. They'd be stunned at his care and precision – everyday cooking elevated to an art form.

My summer holidays, usually spent with my grandparents, who ran a stall in Turin's fruit and vegetable market, also revolved around food. Shopping for ingredients in Italy is a national obsession. The market square is without doubt the hub of social activity. The same scrutinising of fruit and vegetables goes on today as it has done for centuries. Ingredients are discussed and produce picked over until just the right degree of ripeness is found. I discovered this early, when I was allowed to help on the stall, a coveted opportunity to enter the baffling world of grown-ups. It was an important lesson in the first rule of cooking: always start with fresh, top-quality ingredients.

That was then, but it has very much shaped the realisation of a dream long nurtured by my father and me: to take our passion for good food a stage further and market our own sauces. For Vincenzo, with his excellent cooking skills and understanding of good dining, it's important to keep alive old family recipes and see the Dallaglio culinary secrets safely passed on.

I learned my love of cooking from him, picking up techniques while sitting on the kitchen counter, seeing how to follow a recipe, tasting and adjusting flavours. Now the baton has been passed to me, and it's my turn to show Enzo, Ella and Josie that cooking with great ingredients is fun, and doing it as a family even more so.

top left 1995: playing for the England A team.
top right 1980: St Osmunds School photo of me with my sister, Francesca.
middle left Asti, May 2009: lunch with (from left) Lorenzo Ercole (President of Sacla'), me, his daughter Chiara (granddaughter of the founders) and Vincenzo.
middle right September 2009: with Caldicott School boys at a training session, followed by a lunch of pasta and new sauces to celebrate their launch.
bottom left Barnes, London, September 1968: the wedding of my parents, Vincenzo and Eileen.
bottom right Provence, 1988: on holiday with Alice and our eldest daughter, Ella.

Me, aged eight, with my sister Francesca, who tragically died in the sinking of the *Marchioness* on the Thames in 1989. It's the memory of my mother's tireless efforts to get justice for my sister and all the young lives lost on that boat that inspired me to start the Dallaglio Foundation. Our slogan is 'Powerful together', and it does what it says, drawing groups and communities together to work to raise money and provide opportunities for people less fortunate than I am.

Powerful together

Dallaglio Foundation

www.dallagliofoundation.com

There is unquestionable truth in the saying 'You are what you eat'. I believe that my robust good health and ability to withstand the gruelling training regimes and massive energy requirements of playing rugby at world level have been due, in large part, to my excellent diet. That's how the Dallaglio sauces and our slow-baked tomato antipasti came about. My dad and I worked shoulder to shoulder with the Ercole family, owners of Sacla', to produce big-flavoured, big-hearted and health-promoting sauces.

Putting Italian cooking's legendary freshness at the heart of my own growing children's diet is a no-brainer. It's simple, because good ingredients stand best on their own; it's healthy because it's clean and unadulterated. Think about the ingredients that form the backbone of the Italian kitchen and you can see why it's so highly regarded by the medical fraternity worldwide: olive oil, tomatoes, lemons, celery, olives, artichokes, peppers, balsamic vinegar, rice, pasta, polenta, pizza and olive oil breads. The heaviest foods, such as meat, are served last, so it's difficult to over-eat because you haven't any room left. Meals are turned into an event to be shared with family and friends – you chew, talk, chew and talk long into the evening. These principles apply to all good cooking and they underpin the recipes in this book, as well as every single product produced by Sacla'.

Little did we know that when my father and I set out to find the food producer best suited to help us get our ideas to market, our ambition would bring with it the chance to forge the perfect partnership between two Italian families. This relationship has come to have special meaning, because we have such an extraordinary amount in common: our Piedmontese background, a great love of cooking, a passion for the highest quality ingredients, excellent wine, and a deep and abiding love of family and tradition. You only have to sit back and watch Lorenzo Ercole and my dad in the development kitchen in Asti, north-west Italy, or listen to them debating the merits of this tomato or that basil at one of the many joint family lunches, to feel the passion and commitment that has gone into our sauces. It's rare to hook up with people whose values and principles so uncannily mirror your own.

Sacla's success story is heartwarming and it happened for all the right reasons. For us, the fact that it has been owned and run by the same family since it started in 1939, rather than by a faceless, multinational corporation, is hugely important. What's more, the Ercoles come from the same region of Italy, so we have a lot in common. You just get massively more pride, passion and authority from a business whose products are personally controlled by the individuals who own it. We like their spiritedness, their up-for-it attitude and their creative blend of traditional ways with progressive methods. We especially like their ethics – from the way they treat farmers as partners and respect the rhythm of the seasons, to ensuring the lightest possible footprint on the earth and harnessing natural energy to run their operation. Proof of how seriously they take this is that one of their two production sites in Piedmont is powered entirely by the sun. And while we're talking inventive engineering, how many of us know that it was Sacla' who developed the technology to remove the stones from olives? Every time I open a jar of pitted olives I heave a sigh of gratitude.

We care passionately about food, the way it's grown and harvested for our consumption, and the way we cook it. We very much hope that you do, too, and that these recipes will give you and your family as much pleasure as they have given ours, over so many generations.

Finally, I must thank my father Vincenzo, my wife Alice, my children Ella, Josie and Enzo; and the Sacla' family in Italy for their help and support in making this book.

---

top Sydney, 2003: Rugby World Cup final, on the charge in the build-up to Jason Robinson's try.
middle left 1998: playing for Wasps against Gloucester at a very muddy Kingsholm.
middle centre St James's Palace, 2004: with Alice after receiving my MBE from the Queen.
middle right Asti, 2009: Vincenzo shares a joke with Lorenzo Ercole, President of Sacla'.
bottom left Lake Como, 2006: our wedding.
bottom right Asti, 2009: tasting and testing in the development kitchens.

spuntini
light bites

Like yours, my life is hectic. But I've learned that it's when you're flat out that you can't afford to let your diet slide. Here are a few nifty ways of getting the fuel you need without a huge hassle.

fonduta piemontese
fontina cheese fondue

Dad jokes that the Italians invented fondue, not the French. Whatever the truth, this is a family favourite. If you can't get hold of fontina cheese, use mature Cheddar.

Prep time: 5 mins
Cooking time: 5 mins

SERVES 4

INGREDIENTS
300g fontina cheese, chopped
100ml full-fat milk
15g butter
1 tsp plain flour
100ml dry white wine
salt and freshly ground white pepper,
   to season
cubes of bread, toasted

Put the cheese in a bowl and pour over the milk. Leave to soak for a few hours.

Melt the butter in a pan. Stir in the flour and cook for 1 min. Add the milk and cheese and slowly stir everything together.

Pour in the wine, season and simmer for a few minutes. Pour into a fondue dish to keep warm, then serve and let everyone help themselves to the cubes of bread for dipping.

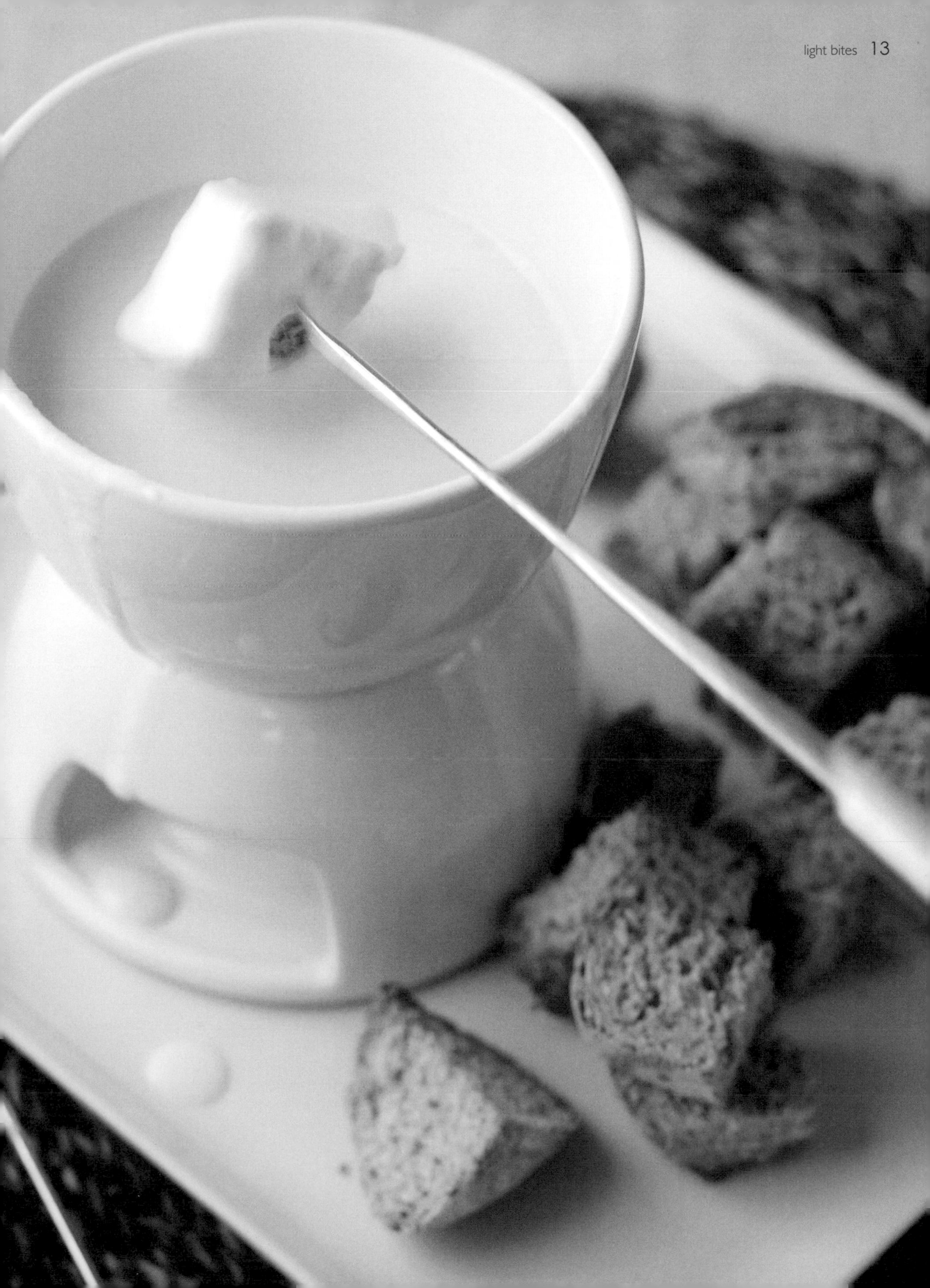

bagna cauda
piedmontese fondue

This recipe takes me back to the rip-roaring, six-hour lunch with the Ercole family at my house to celebrate Dallaglio sauces' first anniversary. *Bagna cauda* happens to be a speciality of Fernanda Ercole, wife of the President of Sacla', so she brought her own recipe over from Italy. It was amazing, but since there's no way she'll divulge hers, you'll have to make do with mine! It's rich and warming, so a little goes a long way.

Prep time: 15 mins
Cooking time: around 20 mins

SERVES 8

INGREDIENTS

2 small garlic cloves, peeled
75ml milk
100g jar anchovies in oil, drained
100ml olive oil
25g unsalted butter, cubed, at room temperature
freshly ground black pepper

For dipping

A selection of raw vegetables: peppers, quartered and deseeded; fennel, outer leaves removed and quartered; celery hearts, quartered; chicory or radicchio, quartered; carrots, peeled and halved lengthways; slices of ciabatta or Italian Pugliese bread

Put the garlic cloves in a small pan with the milk and simmer for 15 mins until soft. Set aside to cool a little.

Place the garlic and the milk in a small blender and whiz to a purée. Add the anchovies next and blend to a thick paste.

Slowly add the oil, dripping it in little by little, as you do when making mayonnaise, making sure that each batch is absorbed before adding the next.

Finally, add the butter, cube by cube, to make a thick, creamy consistency. Season with pepper.

Transfer the *bagna cauda* to a small saucepan to gently warm through – don't let it boil. Stir constantly. Serve with the prepared raw vegetables and lots of bread for dipping.

'This is a real Piedmontese crowd pleaser — serve it up when you've a lot of mouths to feed'

peperoni alla piemontese
marinated peppers with anchovies, garlic and oil

This is one of my favourite ways of cooking peppers – I make it by the bucketload, so there's always some in the fridge for healthy snacking.

Prep time: 15 mins
Cooking time: 20 mins, plus
    marinating time

SERVES 4

INGREDIENTS
3 red or yellow peppers
2 tbsp olive oil
1 garlic clove, peeled and sliced
4 anchovies in oil, drained
1 tbsp capers
salt and freshly ground black pepper

Preheat the grill. Halve the peppers, cut out the core and get rid of the seeds. Place them on a baking sheet skin-side up and grill until blackened all over and the skin starts to peel away.

Tip into an airtight container and seal with the lid. Leave for about 30 mins: the heat from the peppers steams up the container and will make the skin come off more easily.

Peel the peppers and put them in a shallow dish with their juices. Discard the papery skins.

Heat the oil in a small pan with the garlic until you can just begin to smell it. Don't cook it for too long – you don't want it to turn golden, you just want the garlic to release its flavour into the oil.

Pour over the peppers, then snip over the anchovies and scatter over the capers. Season well and toss the ingredients together. Leave to marinate in the fridge for at least 1 hour and up to 24 hours. Make sure you take them out of the fridge around 30 mins before you want to eat them to allow the flavours to develop.

pomodori gratinati
baked tomatoes with breadcrumbs

If you've a glut of tomatoes from your garden, or some that aren't as ripe as they could be, do what the Italians do. Roasting them intensifies the flavour, and when you add garlic and herbs, you make this into a simple starter or easy light lunch.

Prep time: 15 mins
Cooking time: 30–35 mins

SERVES 4

INGREDIENTS
1 slice white bread
4 beef tomatoes, halved horizontally
1–2 tbsp olive oil
1 garlic clove, peeled and crushed
salt and freshly ground black pepper
1 tsp each finely chopped oregano
    and thyme
15g pecorino cheese, freshly grated

Preheat the oven to 200°C/180°C fan oven/gas mark 6.

Chop the bread and put in a small food processor and whiz to make breadcrumbs.

Use a teaspoon to scoop out and discard the seeds from the tomatoes. Put the tomatoes, cut-side up, in a shallow ovenproof dish. Mix together the oil and garlic and season well. Drizzle equally over the tomatoes, making sure the garlic drops into the cavities in the tomatoes.

Mix together the breadcrumbs, herbs and cheese, and season. Sprinkle over the tomatoes and bake in the oven for 30–35 mins until the breadcrumbs start to turn golden and the tomatoes are cooked.

focaccia
italian olive oil bread

This is a typical Italian bread – it's made with more olive oil than you'd normally use in a loaf, but this is what gives it its fantastic moisture.

Prep time: 1 hour 25 mins, including proving time
Cooking time: 30 mins

SERVES 6

INGREDIENTS
25g fresh yeast
500g strong plain flour
1½ tsp salt
3 tbsp olive oil
6 Dallaglio by Sacla' Italian Slow-Baked Tomatoes Marinated With Chilli, chopped, plus some oil from the jar
leaves from a few sprigs of thyme

Put the yeast in 300ml lukewarm water and stir to dissolve. Sift the flour into a large bowl and stir in the salt.

Make a well in the centre and add the olive oil, then pour in the yeast mixture. Stir using a knife, then get stuck in with your hands and knead until the mixture comes together. Put the dough on a board and knead for another 5 mins until smooth and elastic. Don't add more flour – it should be soft and sticky. Put the dough back in a clean bowl, cover and leave for about 45 mins until it has doubled in size.

Dust a board with flour and roll out the dough to make a rectangle of about 30 x 20cm. Line a baking sheet with baking parchment and slide the dough onto it. Leave it in a warm place for about 30 mins to prove – it's ready when you touch it and the soft, pillowy dough springs back.

Now preheat the oven to 200°C/180°C fan oven/gas mark 6. With your fingers, make indents all over the surface. Drizzle with a little chilli oil from the jar, then bake for 20 mins.

Remove from the oven and spoon the chopped oven-baked tomatoes evenly over the bread. Sprinkle over the thyme. Bake for a further 10 mins until the bread sounds hollow when tapped. Cool on a wire rack, then slice it into fingers to serve.

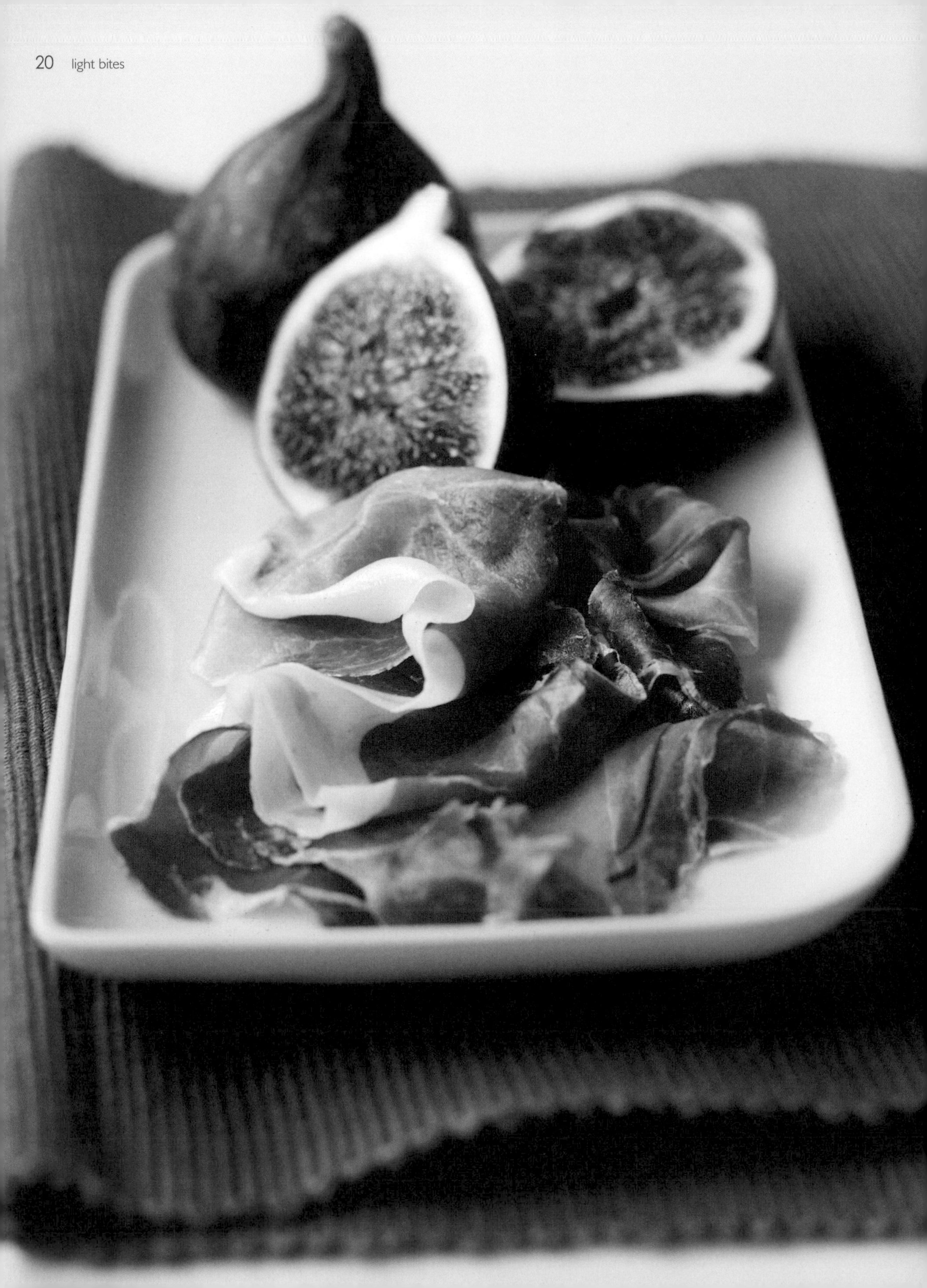

prosciutto san daniele e fichi
fresh figs with prosciutto

Figs wrapped in prosciutto is one of those classic, ultra-simple Italian combinations that relies totally on the quality and flavour of the ingredients. Figs are in season in early autumn, having ripened over the summer. Keep them in the fruit bowl, not the fridge, to enjoy the flavour at its best.

Prep time: 10 mins

SERVES 4

INGREDIENTS
8 slices Prosciutto San Daniele
8 fresh figs

Take the prosciutto out of the fridge 30 mins before serving – the ham should be at room temperature to bring out its full flavour.

Slice the figs in half and serve either with the ham, or wrap half a slice of ham around each fig half. It's as simple as that.

'Summer holidays in Portugal at Maurie and Suzy's farmhouse. Fresh figs from the tree!'

crostini con patè di olive nere
black olive tapenade

You need good-quality olives for this really simple dip, then just add whatever flavouring ingredients take your fancy.

Prep time: 10 mins

SERVES 6

INGREDIENTS
around 170g stoned black olives
½ garlic clove, peeled and crushed
1–2 tbsp olive oil
salt and freshly ground black pepper
1 tsp balsamic vinegar
leaves picked from 2–3 sprigs of thyme

Put the black olives and garlic in a food processor or mini blender with the oil, and whiz to a coarse-textured purée. Spoon into a bowl, season well and stir in the vinegar and thyme. Serve with focaccia or on crostini or bruschetta.

'What I love about Italian food is its simplicity'

funghi ripieni
stuffed mushrooms

Whoever said life's too short to stuff a mushroom didn't think about the man-sized, flat field or portobello ones, which are perfect for filling with ingredients. I like to get a taste of herbs from this dish – it marries well with the earthy flavour of the mushrooms.

Prep time: 10 mins
Cooking time: 20–30 mins

SERVES 4

INGREDIENTS
8 field or portobello mushrooms
125g ricotta cheese
3 spring onions, finely chopped
a couple of sage leaves, finely chopped
salt and freshly ground black pepper
25g Parmesan cheese, freshly grated
2 tsp olive oil, to drizzle

Preheat the oven to 200°C/180°C fan oven/gas mark 6.

Remove the stalk from each mushroom and place flat-side up into a roasting tin. You don't need the stalks for this recipe, but you can save them to use in soups, if you like.

Beat together the ricotta, spring onions and sage, and season well. Stir in half the grated cheese.

Divide the mixture equally among the mushrooms, sprinkle with the remaining cheese and drizzle with a little oil. Cook in the oven for 20–30 mins. Serve with ciabatta bread.

peperonata
mixed pepper medley

This is one of those wonderful recipes so typical of Italian cooking: a sweet vegetable stew that's rich with the natural juices of the peppers. It transforms a handful of ingredients into a lot more than the sum of their parts. Vincenzo, my father, passed this recipe down to me; his mother used to add a chopped potato to the pot, which makes it into a thicker, heartier dish. It tastes even better the day after and will keep for up to five days in the fridge, so I cook double the quantity and use it as a standby. It works well as a starter, goes with any main course and it's really useful when you're trying to perform the miracle of the loaves and fishes, when you unexpectedly find you've got a crowd to feed.

Prep time: 30 mins
Cooking time: 1 hour

SERVES 8

INGREDIENTS
3 tbsp olive oil
1 large onion, peeled and sliced
2 each red, orange and yellow peppers,
  finely sliced
salt and freshly ground black pepper
300g tomatoes, deseeded and chopped

Heat the oil in a pan and add the onion. Cook gently for around 15 mins, until softened. Add the peppers, season well, and cover. Continue to cook slowly over a low heat for 40 mins – there'll be enough liquid in the peppers to make a delicious natural stock.

Add the tomatoes and cook for a further 5 mins.

sacla' tip
For a real zing, add 2 tbsp Dallaglio by Sacla' Diavola sauce.

bruschetta di Vincenzo
Vincenzo's bruschetta

Bruschetta (pronounced with a 'k' rather than with a 'sh') can be topped with whatever takes your fancy. I like to keep it simple and put each topping in its own bowl so that people can help themselves to whatever they like.

Prep time: 15 mins
Cooking time: 5 mins

SERVES 4

INGREDIENTS

6 garlic cloves, peeled
100ml olive oil
ripe tomatoes
extra virgin olive oil
basil leaves
mozzarella, sliced
rocket
Parma ham
8 slices Italian bread (campagnola)

Make the garlic oil by slicing the garlic and putting it in a small pan with the olive oil. Heat gently for a few minutes over a very low heat, making sure the garlic doesn't turn golden, otherwise the flavour will be too strong and bitter. Set aside to cool.

Chop the tomatoes, put them in a bowl and drizzle with the extra virgin olive oil. Tear a few basil leaves and stir in. Put the remaining ingredients in separate bowls.

Lightly toast the bread and brush each slice with the garlic oil. Put on a plate with all the bowls filled with the other ingredients and let everyone make their own. Enjoy!

Sacla' tip

Use Dallaglio by Sacla' Slow-Baked Tomatoes – either the Marinated With Garlic or the Marinated With Chilli. Also, try spreading a little Sacla' Classic Basil Pesto onto bruschetta before layering on the other ingredients.

carpaccio di manzo con rucola e grana

carpaccio of beef with rocket and parmesan

A good carpaccio relies on the quality of the beef, so buy from a good butcher who knows the farm where it was reared. It makes a stunning starter that can either be served on a platter for a big group of people, or on individual plates for a more intimate gathering.

Prep time: 10 mins, plus freezing time of 1 hour, plus 30 mins to reach room temperature

SERVES 4–6

INGREDIENTS
200g beef fillet
100g rocket
chunk of Parmesan cheese
extra virgin olive oil or, if you want to splash out, truffle oil
salt and freshly ground black pepper

Wrap the beef in clingfilm and freeze for about 1 hour.

Remove from the freezer and unwrap the clingfilm. Use a sharp meat knife to slice the beef into very thin rounds. Lay the slices on a plate and set aside for 30 mins to allow them to reach room temperature.

Garnish with the rocket and use a vegetable peeler to shave over enough Parmesan to generously feed four people. Drizzle with whichever oil you prefer and season.

grigliata di verdure
medley of grilled vegetables

This is inspired by a dish we love at Riva in Barnes, south London, our favourite restaurant that doubles as the Dallaglio family canteen. Use whatever vegetables you have to hand, but make sure you griddle them well so that they're properly cooked through. The mint adds a refreshing element and, if you like a kick of heat, use a red chilli instead of a green one.

Prep time: 10 mins
Cooking time: 40 mins

SERVES 4

INGREDIENTS

1 red pepper
1 yellow pepper
2 courgettes
1 aubergine
4 large flat portobello mushrooms
a little olive oil, for brushing
3–4 tbsp extra virgin olive oil
1 mild green chilli, chopped
salt and freshly ground black pepper
a few mint leaves, torn

Start by preparing the vegetables. Halve the peppers and remove the core, seeds and any white pith. Halve again.

Slice the courgettes lengthways. Slice the aubergine lengthways into three or four slices. Trim the stalks of the mushroom and brush off any soil.

Brush all the vegetables with oil and heat a griddle pan until hot. Griddle the vegetables in batches until tender enough to eat.

Transfer to a platter. Put the extra virgin olive oil in a bowl with the chilli and season well. Drizzle over the veg and garnish with the mint.

insalata di arance e finocchio
fennel and orange salad

For a salad to taste its best, take the ingredients out of the fridge a while before serving – they taste better at room temperature. A good dressing makes a salad, so make sure all the ingredients get coated, not just the ones nearest the top. Alice and the girls usually take care of this bit while Enzo and I do 'man's work'.

Prep time: 15 mins

SERVES 4

INGREDIENTS

4 tbsp extra virgin olive oil
1 tbsp white wine vinegar
salt and freshly ground black pepper
1 orange
1 small bulb of fennel
1 small head of radicchio or chicory
8 stoned black olives, halved
small handful of parsley

Put the oil and vinegar in a bowl and season well. Add 1 tsp cold water and whisk briefly.

Use a sharp, serrated knife to cut the top and bottom off the orange, then work around the orange, slicing away the skin and pith. Cut in between each piece of orange skin to extract the segments, and put them in a bowl with their juice.

Finely slice the fennel – use a mandolin if you've got one, but watch you don't slice your fingertips as you get close to the end of the vegetable. Add to the bowl. Separate the leaves of radicchio or chicory and add to the bowl, along with the black olives. Roughly chop the parsley and mix it in. Toss all the ingredients together and serve.

melanzane con pesto e mozzarella
aubergine with pesto and mozzarella

These are great as a lunchtime snack, but they're also smart enough to be part of an antipasto starter. You often hear people say that it's not necessary to salt aubergines, but I disagree: by drawing out the juices, the aubergines will absorb less fat when you fry them.

Prep time: 10 mins, plus salting time
Cooking time: 15 mins

SERVES 4

INGREDIENTS
1 aubergine
salt and freshly ground black pepper
2 tbsp olive oil
1–2 tbsp Sacla' Sun-dried Tomato Pesto
125g mozzarella, sliced

Slice the aubergine into eight rounds. Arrange the slices in a colander, sprinkling each layer with salt. Set aside for 20 mins to allow the salt to draw out the bitter juices. Rinse well.

Heat half the oil and fry the aubergine slices in two batches until golden on each side, adding the remaining oil to the second batch. Spread out on a baking sheet, spread a little pesto on top of each round and top with a slice of mozzarella. Grill until golden.

affettati misti con cipolline in agrodolce
sweet 'n' sour onions

Baby onions and shallots are a pain to peel – the papery skins stick to the bulb and it takes forever to remove the layers. I've found the quickest way is to tip them into a large bowl, cover with boiling water and leave them for about 5–10 minutes. When you drain the water, the skins come away easily. Job done.

Prep time: 15 mins
Cooking time: around 40 mins

SERVES 4

INGREDIENTS
2 tbsp olive oil
400g baby onions or shallots, peeled
2 garlic cloves, peeled and sliced
3 tbsp light muscovado sugar
200ml red wine vinegar
1 tsp finely chopped rosemary

Heat the oil in a small saucepan and cook the whole onions over a low heat until very soft, stirring every now and then for about 20 mins. Add a splash of water if the mixture looks dry.

Add the garlic and cook for 1–2 mins. Stir in the sugar, vinegar and rosemary, and bring to the boil. Cook, covered, for about 15 mins.

Remove the lid and continue to simmer until syrupy.

Serve with...
Affettati misti – a traditional plate of mixed, cured meats. If you have a good Italian deli nearby, ask them to give you a varied selection. It should be made up a bit like a cheese board, with a choice of different meats. I like to include a spicy salami and finocchiona, which is Tuscan salami made with fennel seeds.

impasto di piadina alla Dallaglio
Dallaglio's doughballs

I used to make these with my grandmother in Italy, then with my dad in London. Now it's my son Enzo's turn, and he loves making them. They're dead easy to make and ready for the oven as soon as the dough is shaped into balls. Plus, they cook really fast, which is a bonus as far as Enzo's concerned.

Prep time: 30 mins, plus rising and proving time
Cooking time: 10–12 mins

SERVES 4

INGREDIENTS
10g fresh yeast
300g strong plain flour
½ tsp salt
1 tsp olive oil
75g softened butter
1 garlic clove, peeled and crushed
1 tsp each chopped parsley and chives

sacla' tip
Warm half a jar of Dallaglio by Sacla' Napoletana sauce in a pan and serve alongside the doughballs.

Line a baking sheet with baking parchment. Put the yeast in a bowl and pour over 90ml lukewarm water.

Sift the flour into a separate bowl, stir in the salt and make a well in the centre. Pour in the yeast mixture, followed by another 90ml lukewarm water and the oil. Mix with a knife, then get your hands in there and bring the mixture together. Put the dough on a board and knead well. Resist adding any more flour – it should be soft and sticky. Set aside for 30 mins to rise.

Divide the dough into quarters, then divide each quarter into four or five pieces. Roll into small balls and place on the prepared baking sheet. Repeat with the remaining dough.

Preheat the oven to 200°C/180°C fan oven/gas mark 6. Bake for 10–12 mins until pale golden. The doughballs are ready when they sound hollow when tapped on the base.

In a bowl, beat together the butter, garlic and herbs. Season well. Serve with the doughballs.

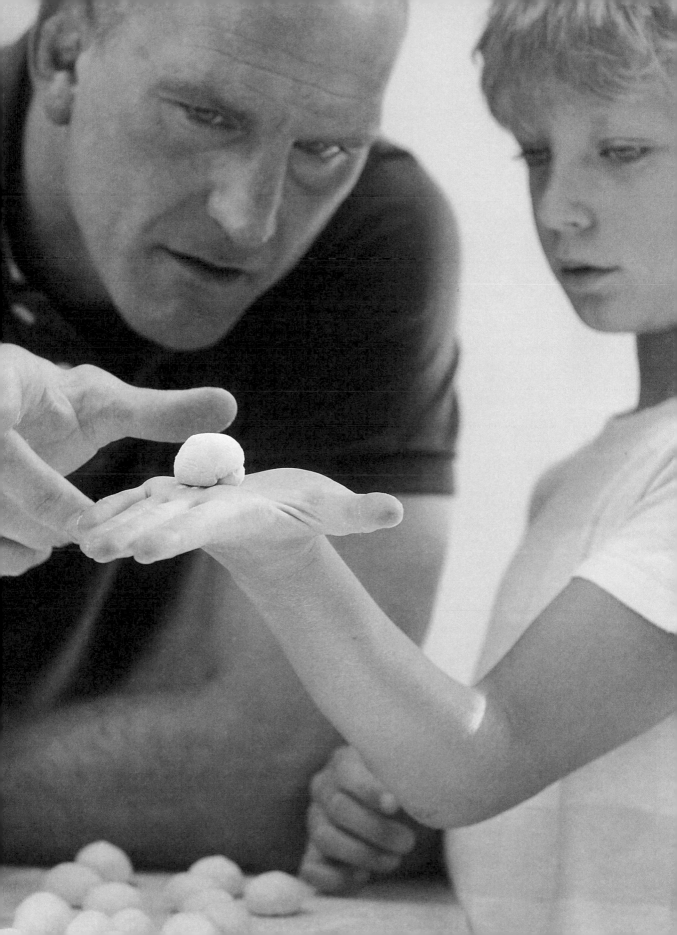

torta di pancetta e parmigiano
savoury pancetta muffins

This is a speedy recipe that you can make with the family. Serve it for brunch with eggs, beans and mushrooms, or as an afternoon snack. Add herbs if you like, but I've used my favourite ready-made pesto, which gives it a savoury punch.

Prep time: 15 mins
Cooking time: 25–30 mins

MAKES 6 MUFFINS

INGREDIENTS
100g pancetta
225g self-raising flour
50g Parmesan cheese, freshly grated
½ tsp salt
40g butter, melted and cooled
175g natural yoghurt
1 medium egg
2 tbsp Sacla' Organic Tomato Pesto

You'll need a six-hole muffin tin and six paper muffin cases; or a silicone muffin mould (which needs no lining).

Preheat the oven to 200°C/180°C fan oven/gas mark 6.

Put the pancetta in a frying pan and dry fry over a medium heat. Cook until golden and crispy. Tip onto a sheet of kitchen paper to drain any fat and leave to cool.

Put the flour, Parmesan and salt in a bowl. Add the cooled pancetta and toss together to mix.

In a separate bowl, beat together the cooled butter, yoghurt, egg and pesto. Make a well in the centre of the flour mixture and pour in the yoghurt mixture. Roughly mix together – there should still be some floury patches, but don't worry, it's meant to be like that.

Spoon into the muffin tin, piling the mixture high in each hole. Bake for 25–30 mins or until a skewer pushed into the middle comes out clean.

Remove from the tin and cool on a wire rack until just warm, then dive in.

vova alla fiorentina
eggs florentine

You'll find lots of recipes for eggs Florentine, but no one does it better than the Italians, who stick to the simplest form. There isn't any hollandaise or béchamel sauce; it's just spinach sautéed in butter, topped with an egg and baked in the oven. If you want to give the spinach a flavour boost, this is the time to use up any leftover sauces.

Prep time: 10 mins
Cooking time: 20 mins

SERVES 4

INGREDIENTS
500g spinach
15g butter
salt and freshly ground black pepper
4 medium eggs

Preheat the oven to 200°C/180°C fan oven/gas mark 6.

Wash the spinach well and shake off the excess water. Melt the butter in a pan and add the spinach. Season well, cover with a lid and cook for a few minutes until just wilted – you may need to toss it halfway through.

Divide the spinach among four shallow ovenproof dishes. Make a little well in the centre and crack an egg into each. Season, then bake in the oven for 15–17 mins until the egg is cooked but the yolk is still runny.

Sacla' tip
Add a little Dallaglio by Sacla' Napoletana sauce to the spinach.

'My dad Vincenzo, aged 8, with his two sisters, Giuseppina and Ernestina, at his First Holy Communion in 1941'

caponata siciliana
sicilian aubergine stew

Italians love vegetable stews and this one, with its rich aubergines, is a favourite among meat-lovers. It's an unusual dish, because it uses vinegar to give it sharpness, which is then balanced with sugar. Again, it improves with a day in the fridge to allow all the flavours to come together.

Prep time: 10 mins
Cooking time: 30 mins

SERVES 4

INGREDIENTS

2 large aubergines, chopped into chunks
2 tbsp olive oil
1 onion, peeled and chopped
2 sticks of celery, chopped
400g can chopped tomatoes
1 tsp caster sugar
2–3 tbsp red wine vinegar
50g pitted black olives

Put the chopped aubergine in a colander and sprinkle with salt. Set aside for 1 hour to extract the bitter juices. Rinse well.

Heat the oil in a large pan. Fry the onion on a low heat until softened, for about 10–15 mins. Add the celery and aubergine and cook for a further 5 mins.

Tip in the tomatoes and stir everything together. Add the sugar, vinegar and olives, cover with a lid and simmer for about 15 mins until reduced and sauce-like in texture.

frittelle di zucchine
courgette fritters

This recipe is very simple to make and tastes out of this world. You only need one courgette to make enough fritters for four people, so it takes hardly any time to prepare. Make sure you season the mixture, though, as courgettes can be bland. Sometimes I add a bit of lemon zest or a grating of nutmeg, which complements courgette well.

Prep time: 15 mins
Cooking time: 15 mins

SERVES 4

INGREDIENTS
1 medium egg
25g plain flour
salt and freshly ground black pepper
30g pecorino cheese, freshly grated
1 large courgette, grated
a couple of sage leaves, finely chopped
2 tsp olive oil

Beat together the egg and flour and season well. If you have time, set the mixture aside for 30 mins to allow the flour to be absorbed into the egg. Fold in the pecorino, grated courgette and sage.

Heat the oil in a frying pan and drop three or four tablespoonfuls of the mixture into it. Fry for a few minutes over a medium heat until golden, then turn over and cook on the other side. Repeat with the remaining mixture and serve immediately.

insalata di tonno e fagioli
tuna and bean salad

Italians are very fussy about the quality of their ingredients, and it particularly shows in their salads. For this one, you need to buy really good tuna — preserved in extra virgin olive oil — to get the best flavour.

Prep time: 15 mins

SERVES 4

INGREDIENTS

½ red onion, peeled and finely chopped
1 tbsp red wine vinegar
115g can tuna preserved in olive oil, drained
400g can cannellini beans, drained
1 tbsp capers
2 tbsp freshly chopped parsley
salt and freshly ground black pepper
4 Dallaglio by Sacla' Slow-Baked Tomatoes Marinated With Garlic, sliced
50g rocket
2 tbsp extra virgin olive oil

Put the onion in a little bowl with a pinch of salt and the vinegar. Toss well and set aside to marinate.

Put the drained tuna in a large salad bowl. Add the beans, capers and parsley and toss well. Season to taste.

Stir in the sliced tomatoes and rocket. Add the extra virgin olive oil to the red onion mixture and mix well. Pour over the salad, toss and serve.

prosciutto con finocchio al forno
baked fennel with parma ham

Poaching the fennel first in a little vegetable stock softens the wonderful aniseed flavour. Then it gets star treatment with a bit of cream, ricotta and Parma ham. This dish is pretty versatile: I serve it as a hot starter if we have friends round, and it's easily adjusted to suit vegetarians – just leave out the ham and scatter over freshly grated Parmesan instead. Make sure you've got plenty of crusty bread to go round.

Prep time: 10 mins
Cooking time: 20 mins

SERVES 4

INGREDIENTS

2 large fennel bulbs
200ml hot vegetable stock
50ml double cream
50g ricotta cheese
salt and freshly ground black pepper
4 slices Parma ham

Preheat the oven to 200°C/180°C fan oven/gas mark 6.

Cut each fennel bulb lengthways into four thick slices. Cut off the green fronds and reserve. Put the bulbs in a pan with the hot stock, cover and bring to the boil, then simmer for 5 mins until tender.

Lift out and transfer to an ovenproof dish. Stir the cream and ricotta into the stock in the pan and season well, then pour it over the fennel and place the Parma ham slices on top. Cook in the oven for 15 mins, by which time the sauce will be bubbling and the Parma ham crisp. Chop the reserved fronds and scatter on top.

piatti rapidi durante la settimana
quick weekday suppers

Organising the family and keeping on top of the hundred and one fixtures that dominate our household sometimes feels like herding cats. But we never stint on good, nutritious, weeknight food.

2

polpette alla diavola
meatballs with diavola sauce

This is a great basic way of making meatballs. If you prefer, you can use the mince mixture to make four hearty burgers and serve them in a bun with a dollop of the sauce.

Prep time: 15 mins
Cooking time: 15 mins

SERVES 4

INGREDIENTS

500g lean beef mince
1 tbsp freshly chopped parsley
1 tbsp freshly chopped basil
4 spring onions, chopped
zest of 1 lemon
100g breadcrumbs
pinch of ground cinnamon
salt and freshly ground black pepper
a little olive oil
300g jar Dallaglio by Sacla'
   Diavola sauce
400g penne pasta
freshly grated Parmesan cheese

Bring a large pan of salted water to the boil.

Put the mince in a bowl with the herbs, spring onions, lemon zest, breadcrumbs and cinnamon. Mix it all together and season well.

Take walnut-sized pieces of the mince and roll into balls. Heat a little olive oil in a pan and fry the meatballs lightly until golden.

Heat the sauce in a pan and add the meatballs.

Meanwhile, cook the penne in the boiling water until al dente. Add a ladleful of pasta water to the sauce and meatballs – this will loosen the mixture and help bring all the flavours together.

Drain the pasta well. Return it to the pan and add the meatballs and sauce. Toss everything together. Divide among four bowls, sprinkle with Parmesan and serve immediately.

linguine con zucchine
linguine with courgettes

This is a classic from southern Italy and is incredibly quick to make. It's as simple as flavouring the oil with garlic first, then frying the slices of courgette in the oil.

Prep time: 10 mins
Cooking time: 20 mins

SERVES 4

INGREDIENTS

2 tbsp olive oil
2 garlic cloves, peeled and thinly sliced
4 small courgettes, thinly sliced
400g linguine
freshly grated Parmesan cheese
salt and freshly ground black pepper

Bring a large pan of salted water to the boil.

Heat 1 tbsp of the oil in a large pan and gently cook the garlic until soft. Lift out and set aside on a plate.

Add half the courgettes to the pan, spreading them out in an even layer, and fry until golden on each side, seasoning with salt as you go. Lift out onto the plate with the garlic. Pour the remaining tbsp oil into the pan and cook the rest of the courgettes.

Meanwhile, cook the linguine until al dente. Drain the pasta, leaving a little water clinging to the strands. Return to the pan and add the fried courgettes and garlic. Toss all the ingredients together and divide among four bowls.

Sprinkle with Parmesan and serve immediately with a little freshly ground pepper, if you like.

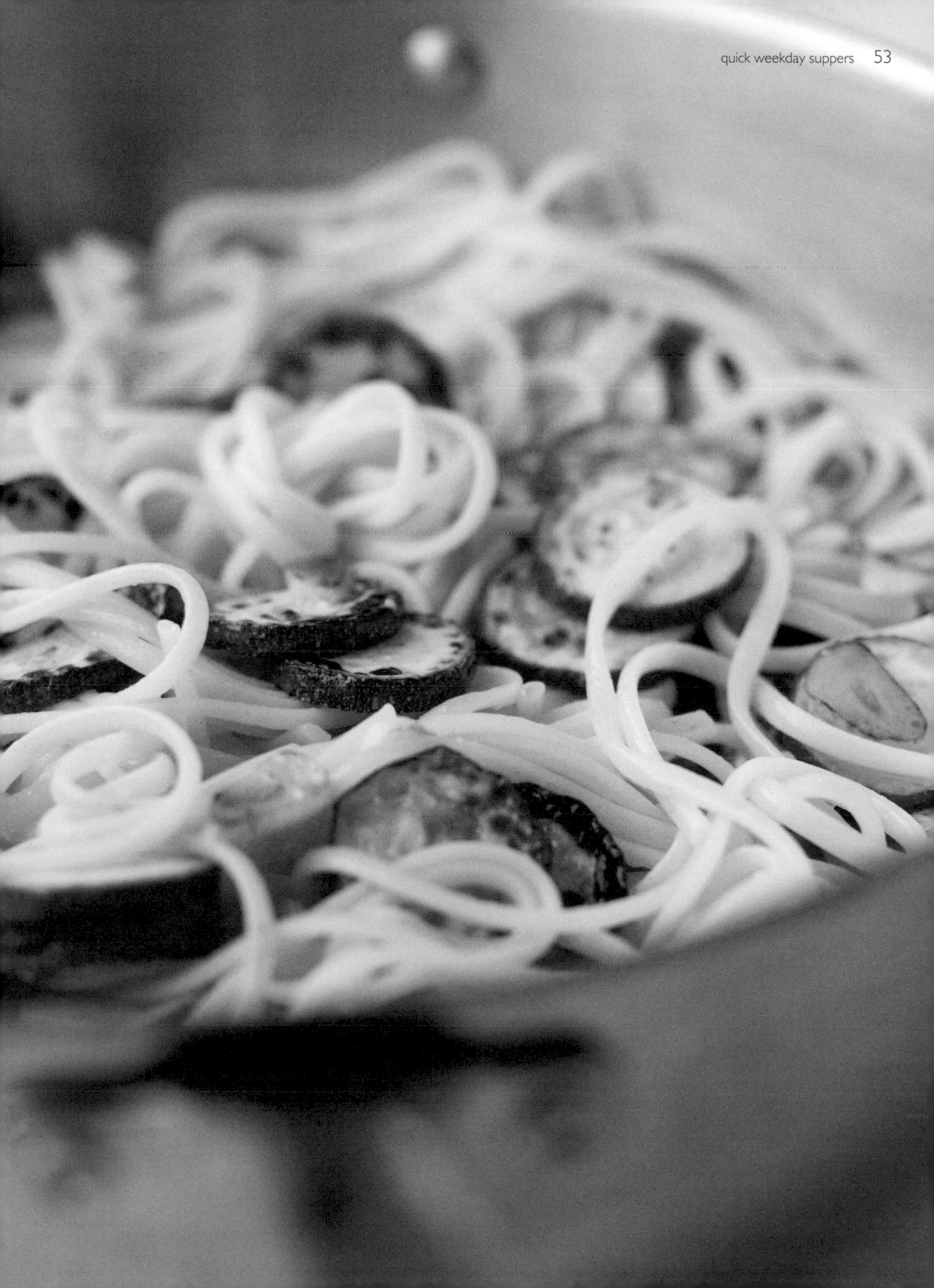

spaghettini all'amatriciana
spaghettini with tomato and bacon sauce

This differs from arrabbiata in that it includes pancetta. Once you've fried the pancetta, make sure you drain the fat away, otherwise the sauce could be a bit greasy. I've used spaghettini here because, for me, it feels a bit lighter.

Prep time: 15 mins
Cooking time: 15 mins

SERVES 4

INGREDIENTS
70g pancetta, cut into small cubes
2 tsp olive oil
1 small garlic clove, peeled and crushed
pinch of chilli flakes
50ml dry white wine
400g can chopped plum tomatoes
salt and freshly ground black pepper
400g spaghettini
a few chopped basil leaves
freshly grated pecorino cheese

Bring a large pan of salted water to the boil.

Heat a frying pan and dry fry the pancetta – you won't need oil, as there's enough fat from the meat. When it's cooked, drain off the fat and place on kitchen paper.

Heat the oil in a pan and gently fry the garlic and chilli flakes until you can just smell the aroma of the garlic cooking in the pan. Add the wine and cook until it has reduced by about half. Tip in the pancetta and tomatoes and season well. Bring to the boil and cook the sauce quickly, adding a ladleful of water to the sauce.

Meanwhile, cook the spaghettini until al dente. Drain the pasta, leaving a little water clinging to the strands. Return to the pan, add half the sauce and stir well, then divide among four plates and top with the remaining sauce and pecorino.

orecchiette con broccoletti e alici
pasta with broccoli, chilli and anchovies

Packed with vegetables, this is a healthy and well-balanced dish. The anchovies give it a tangy saltiness, while the chilli lends a cheeky kick. *Orecchiette* means 'little ears', a perfect shape for trapping and holding the ingredients.

Prep time: 5 mins
Cooking time: 15 mins

SERVES 4

INGREDIENTS
1 small tin anchovies in oil, chopped
1 garlic clove, peeled and sliced
pinch of chilli flakes
½ red pepper, deseeded and chopped
2 plum tomatoes, chopped
400g dried orecchiette pasta
1 head of broccoli
½ lemon, cut into 4 wedges, to serve

Sacla' tip
Save time and use a 300g jar of Dallaglio by Sacla' Diavola sauce instead of tomatoes and pepper.

Heat about 1 tbsp oil from the anchovy tin (discard the rest) in a pan and add the garlic and chilli flakes. Cook for 1 min. Add the red pepper and tomatoes. Heat gently, then add the anchovies and allow them to melt into the sauce.

Bring a large pan of salted water to the boil and cook the orecchiette until al dente. Cut the broccoli into florets and peel the stem, discarding the tough skin. Chop the stem into bite-sized chunks.

About 4 mins before the end of the pasta cooking time, add a ladleful of water to the pepper, tomato and anchovy sauce, then drop the broccoli florets into the pan with the pasta. Cook until the pasta is al dente.

Drain the pasta and broccoli well. Return to the pan and pour in the sauce. Toss together, then divide among four bowls and serve with a wedge of lemon to squeeze over.

gnocchi ripieni di ricotta e spinaci
ricotta and spinach dumplings

If you're thinking that all this spinach makes these dumplings a bit dull and worthy, you'd be wrong. Mixed together with ricotta and lemon, they are transformed into bite-sized angel food. Serve with a drizzle of melted butter, Parmesan and plenty of freshly ground black pepper.

Prep time: 20 mins
Cooking time: 15 mins

SERVES 4

INGREDIENTS
500g spinach
250g ricotta cheese
zest of 1 lemon
1 medium egg, lightly beaten
1 tsp salt
50g plain flour, plus extra for dusting
melted butter and freshly grated Parmesan
   cheese, to serve

Lightly cook the spinach, drain it well and squeeze as much of the water out as possible. Allow to cool.

Roughly chop the spinach and put it in a bowl with the ricotta, lemon zest, egg and salt. Mix everything together, adding the flour, to bring all the ingredients together.

Take walnut-sized pieces of the mixture and roll into balls, using a little flour.

Bring a large pan of salted water to the boil and add the dumplings in batches. When you first drop them in they'll sink to the bottom, but when they're cooked they'll rise to the top and float there – lift them out with a slotted spoon and set aside until you've cooked all of them. Divide among four plates, drizzle with melted butter and top with grated Parmesan.

sacla' tip
You can also bake this dish. Put the dumplings in an overproof dish, spoon over Dallaglio by Sacla' Tricolore sauce, top with 2–3 tbsp breadcrumbs and bake in a hot oven until bubbling and golden.

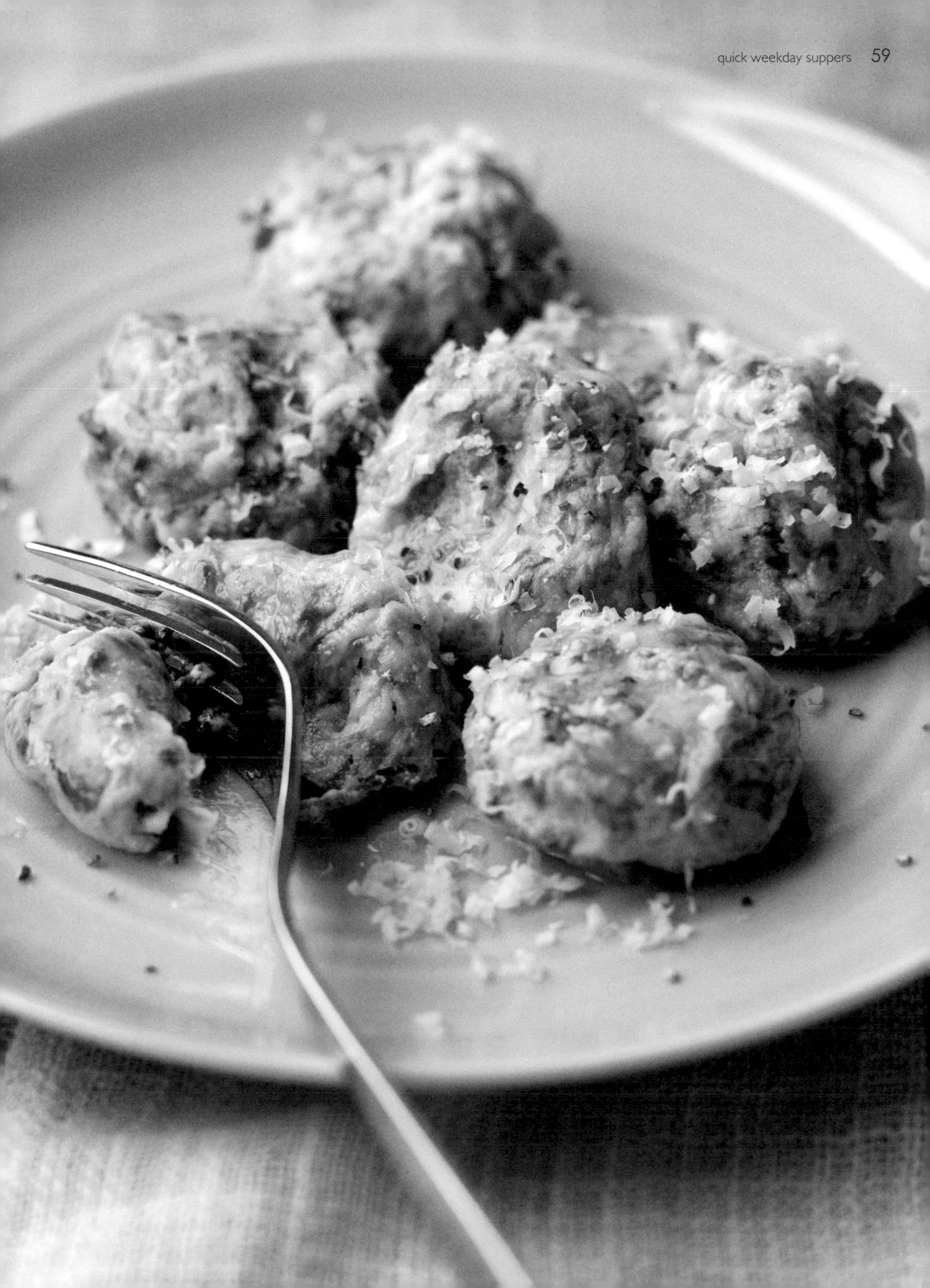

tagliatelle con gorgonzola e noci
gorgonzola and walnut tagliatelle

This is as quick as it gets to rustle up a cooked supper – it's done while the pasta's cooking. The strong, punchy flavour comes from the Italian blue-veined cheese, Gorgonzola, while crunchy nuts give it a bit of attitude. Serve it with plenty of freshly ground black pepper.

Prep and cooking time: 10 mins

SERVES 4

INGREDIENTS
400g tagliatelle
200g Gorgonzola cheese
25g butter
25g walnuts, roughly chopped
2 tbsp freshly chopped parsley
salt and freshly ground black pepper

Bring a large pan of salted water to the boil and cook the tagliatelle until al dente, following the timings on the pack – it's usually around 10 mins.

Chop the cheese and put it in a small pan. Heat gently until half melted – it will continue to melt once you toss it into the pasta.

Drain the pasta, leaving a little water clinging to the pasta. Return it to the pan and add the butter. Toss well, stir in the cheese, nuts and parsley and season well. Divide among four bowls and serve immediately.

'It's taken a while to get the kids to love Gorgonzola as much as Alice and I do...'

stufato di verdure alla ligure
italian-style ratatouille

This tastes even better the day after. You need a wide pan so that the vegetables have a chance to cook first in the oil and don't lie on top of one another and sweat. Cooking the veg in stages may look like more trouble than it's worth, but it allows you to sauté each batch, which maximises the flavour in the finished dish. It's fantastic with a roast.

Prep time: 20 mins, plus salting time
Cooking time: around 45 mins

SERVES 4

INGREDIENTS

1 aubergine, chopped into chunks
2–3 tbsp olive oil
1 onion, peeled and sliced
1 garlic clove, peeled and sliced
1 red pepper, deseeded and chopped
1 large courgette, chopped
200g can chopped tomatoes
1 tbsp tomato purée
200ml hot vegetable stock
2 bay leaves
salt and freshly ground black pepper
1 tsp balsamic vinegar
handful of basil leaves

Put the chopped aubergine in a colander and sprinkle with salt. Set aside for 30 mins to extract the bitter juices. Rinse well.

Heat half the oil in a wide saucepan and sauté the onion for 10 mins over a medium heat until softened. Add the garlic and cook for 1 min. Add the aubergine to the pan with the remaining oil. Cook for a further 10 mins until golden all over.

Add the pepper and courgette and cook for 5 mins, then add the tomatoes, tomato purée, hot stock and bay leaves. Season well. Cover and bring to the boil, then turn the heat down to a simmer and cook for 15–20 mins. Whip the bay leaves out and discard. Add the vinegar to the pan, then roughly tear the basil leaves, stir in and serve.

gnocchi alla diavola
gnocchi and tomato bake

This is comfort food at its best. Homemade gnocchi require just two ingredients – potatoes and flour   so easy that my kids can make them, and much lighter than the ones you buy in the supermarket. Season the dough well, otherwise the gnocchi will taste bland. I like mine in a spicy sauce, so once they're ready, I spoon over my Diavola sauce and sprinkle them with Parmesan.

Prep time: 35 mins, plus 1 hour chilling
Cooking time: 35 mins

SERVES 4

INGREDIENTS
650g floury potatoes, such as King
    Edwards, peeled
½ tsp salt
250g plain flour, plus extra to dust
300g jar Dallaglio by Sacla' Diavola
    sauce
freshly ground black pepper
freshly grated Parmesan cheese

Chop the potatoes into small chunks and steam them until tender. Lift the steamer, place the potato chunks in a bowl and set aside to dry for a few minutes.

Press the potatoes through a potato ricer into a bowl, or mash very thoroughly. Season with the salt and add the flour gradually, stirring it in with a wooden spoon to make a smooth, firm dough. This is like making bread – you might not need to add all the flour, so add it a little at a time. Put the dough on a board and roll it in your hands to make a sausage shape, then wrap it in clingfilm and chill for 1 hour.

Bring a large pan of salted water to the boil. Pour the Diavola sauce into a separate pan and heat gently. Preheat the oven to 200°C/180°C fan oven/gas mark 6.

Unwrap the dough and place it on a board. Dust lightly with a little flour to stop it sticking, then cut off a quarter. Roll this into a sausage shape a little thicker than your thumb, then cut off pieces the length of a finger. Repeat with the rest of the dough until you have a board full of little gnocchi.

Drop about 10 gnocchi into the pan of boiling water in one go and cook in batches. They're ready when they float to the top. Lift out with a slotted spoon and place in an ovenproof dish. Cover each batch with a spoonful of sauce and a little grated Parmesan, seasoning as you go. Continue until all the gnocchi are cooked and all the sauce is used. Bake in the preheated oven for about 10 mins until hot.

pasta alla ligure
italian riviera-style pasta

The traditional pasta to use for this dish is trofie. If you can't get hold of it, use shell-shaped conchiglie or linguine, which catch the pesto sauce well.

Prep time: 5 mins
Cooking time: 10 mins

SERVES 4

INGREDIENTS

400g trofie, conchiglie or linguine
2 medium salad or waxy potatoes,
    peeled and chopped
150g green beans, trimmed and halved
120g Sacla' Classic Basil Pesto
salt and freshly ground black pepper
freshly grated Parmesan cheese

Bring a large pan of salted water to the boil and cook the pasta according to the timings on the pack.

After half the cooking time, add the potatoes and green beans to the pan, cover and bring to the boil again. Remove the lid and continue to cook for the allotted time or until the pasta is al dente. Drain, leaving a little of the cooking water clinging to the pasta. Add the pesto, season and toss all the ingredients together.

Divide among four bowls and grate over a little Parmesan before serving.

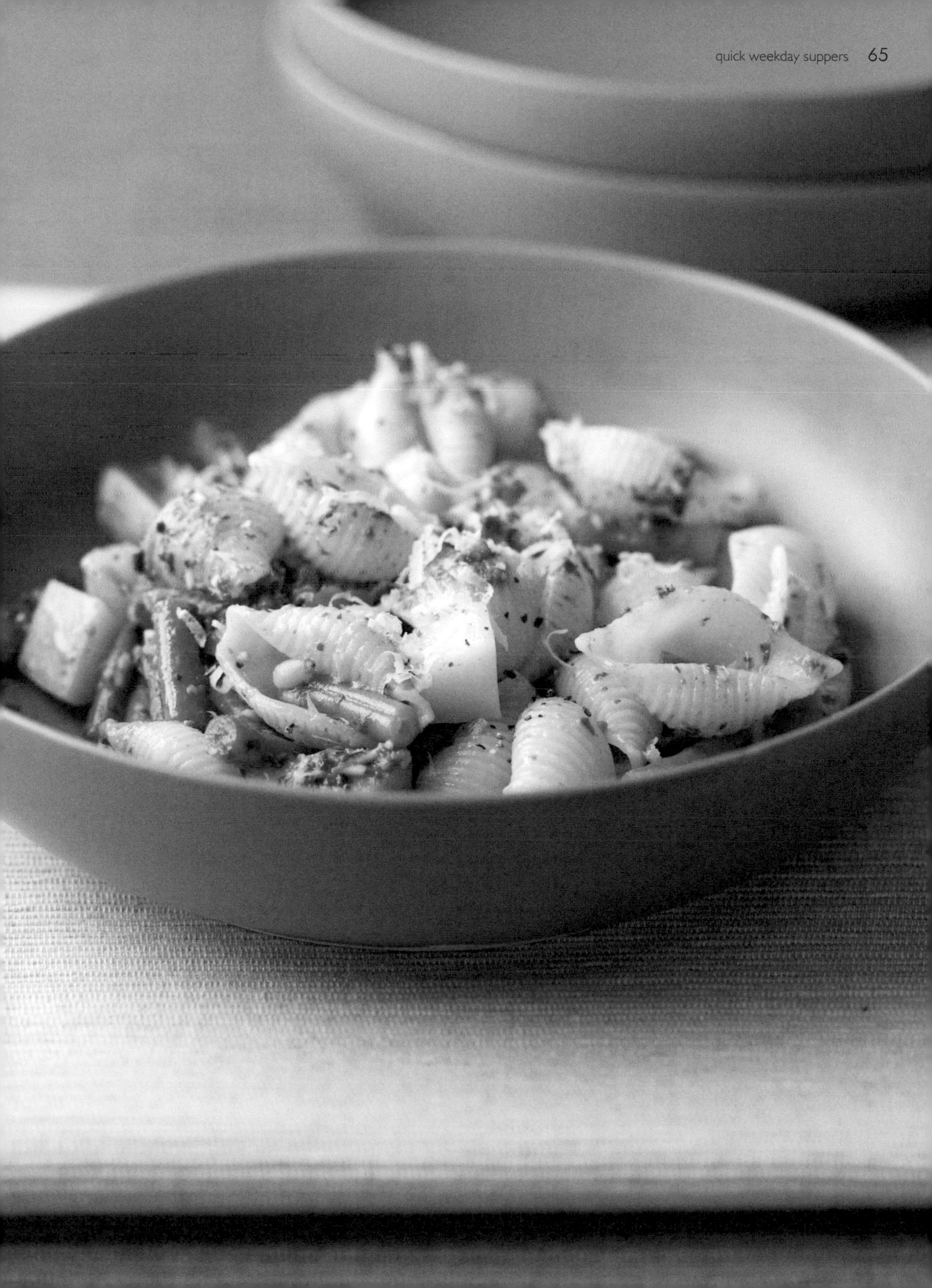

risotto primavera
risotto with peas and asparagus

Italian food is a celebration of the seasons, which is why this recipe is so typical: it brings together all the late spring vegetables just as they're starting to appear in the shops and on market stalls.

Prep time: 15 mins
Cooking time: 30 mins

SERVES 4

INGREDIENTS
1 tbsp olive oil, plus extra for frying
25g butter
1 large onion, peeled and finely chopped
1.4 litres hot chicken stock
400g Arborio risotto rice
100ml dry white wine
salt
150g fresh peas
325g fresh asparagus spears,
    roughly chopped
freshly grated Parmesan cheese

Heat the oil and butter in a pan and cook the onion over a low heat until softened – this will take around 15–20 mins.

Pour the hot stock into a pan and bring to a gentle simmer.

Stir the rice into the onion and cook for 1 min. Pour in the white wine and allow it to reduce, then with the stock just simmering, add it ladleful by ladleful, stirring it into the rice to allow it to be absorbed. Continue to cook, adding the stock slowly, until it has all been absorbed by the rice, seasoning it along the way.

While the rice is cooking, put a little water in a pan and steam the peas. Drain and set aside. In a separate pan, gently fry the asparagus in a little oil until tender.

When the rice is cooked, stir in the peas and asparagus, then divide among four bowls and top each with a little freshly grated Parmesan.

Sacla' tip
Stir two finely chopped Sacla' Artichoke Antipasti into the risotto at the end.

rigatoni alla puttanesca
tart's pasta

There are as many recipes for this particular pasta sauce as there are regions in Italy. As the name suggests, it's big-hearted, rough and ready, so the flavours are accordingly bold and punchy.

Prep time: 10 mins
Cooking time: 15 mins

SERVES 4

INGREDIENTS

1 tbsp olive oil
2 garlic cloves, peeled and roughly
   chopped
4 anchovies in olive oil
pinch of chilli flakes
10 black olives, chopped
1 tbsp capers
400g can chopped tomatoes
salt and freshly ground black pepper
400g rigatoni
2 tbsp freshly chopped parsley

Heat the oil in a shallow pan and add the garlic, anchovies and chilli flakes. Heat gently to allow the anchovies to melt into the oil and the garlic to gently release its flavour.

Stir in the black olives, capers and chopped tomatoes. Season well, bring to the boil and simmer for 15 mins.

Bring a large pan of salted water to the boil. Cook the rigatoni until al dente. Add a ladleful of pasta water to the pan to loosen the sauce. Drain the pasta well, return to the pan and add a little olive oil. Add the sauce and the parsley, and adjust the seasoning if necessary. Toss everything together, then divide among four bowls and serve.

pasta e ceci
chickpea and pasta stew

Here's the fast version of this very old peasant dish. I've fiddled with the recipe for reasons of 'health by stealth', to make sure I get a wide enough range of vegetables into the kids – that's why I use peppers, too.

Prep time: 15 mins
Cooking time: 25 mins

SERVES 4

INGREDIENTS

2 tbsp olive oil
1 onion, peeled and chopped
1 large carrot, peeled and chopped
1 celery stick, chopped
½ garlic clove, peeled and crushed
1 yellow pepper, deseeded and chopped
pinch of chilli flakes
1 sprig of rosemary
400g can chickpeas, drained
200g can chopped tomatoes
2 tsp tomato purée
500ml hot vegetable stock
1 bay leaf
salt and freshly ground black pepper
100g small-shaped pasta for soups
freshly grated Parmesan cheese and
    extra virgin olive oil, to serve

Heat the oil in a pan and add the onion, carrot and celery. Cook for about 10–15 mins until the vegetables have softened. Add the garlic, pepper, chilli flakes and rosemary, and stir in and cook for a further 5 mins.

Add the chickpeas, tomatoes, tomato purée, hot stock and bay leaf. Season well. Cover, bring to the boil, then simmer for 10 mins. Add the pasta to the pan and stir. Cover again and cook the pasta until al dente over a low heat for the time stated on the pack.

Divide among four bowls and serve with the grated Parmesan and a generous drizzle of oil.

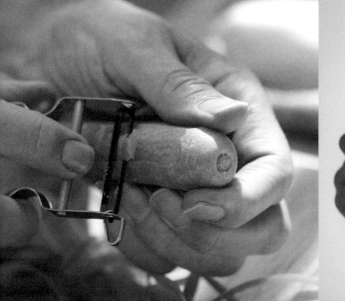

ragù alla bolognese
spaghettini bolognese

The traditional pasta for this sauce is tagliatelle, but my father uses spaghettini, a thinner version of spaghetti. It's lighter than egg pasta and the sauce coats it beautifully. We make double the amount of sauce, with the intention of freezing some, but it has yet to make it as far as the freezer.

Prep time: 30 mins
Cooking time: 45 mins

SERVES 4

INGREDIENTS

2 tbsp vegetable oil or olive oil
1 large onion, peeled and finely chopped
2 sticks of celery, finely chopped
2 medium carrots, peeled and finely chopped
500g beef mince
100g chopped rindless pancetta
1 garlic clove, peeled and chopped
100ml red wine
300ml passata
400g can chopped tomatoes
1 tsp tomato purée
1 beef stock cube
bouquet garni (a bay leaf, a few parsley stalks, a few sprigs of thyme)
dash of Worcestershire sauce
pinch of demerara sugar
salt and freshly ground black pepper
400g spaghettini
basil leaves
freshly grated Parmesan cheese

Sacla' tip

Vincenzo's famous bolognese was the inspiration behind the delicious Dallaglio by Sacla' Bolognese sauce. If time is tight, just brown the mince in a pan, then add the jar of sauce and simmer for 10 mins.

Heat 1 tbsp of the oil in a large saucepan and fry the onion, celery and carrots – this base mixture is what the Italians call the *soffrito*. Cook gently until softened.

In a separate pan, heat the remaining tbsp oil and cook the mince, turning it every now and then until browned and golden.

In another pan, dry fry the pancetta – you won't need any oil as pancetta has enough fat in it already.

When the *soffrito* has softened, stir in the garlic and cook for 1 min.

Drain the mince through a sieve that's resting over a bowl. Add it to the *soffrito*. Do the same with the pancetta and add it to the pan. Discard the fat from both.

Add 50ml wine to each pan in which the mince and pancetta have been cooking to deglaze the pans, then add the juices to the pan with the mince mixture.

Add the passata, the chopped tomatoes, the tomato purée and the beef stock cube with the bouquet garni and 200ml water to the mince. Stir together with the Worcestershire sauce and the sugar. Season well and bring to a gentle simmer, cooking, uncovered, for 30 mins.

Bring a large pan of salted water to the boil. Add the spaghettini and cook until al dente. Add a ladleful of pasta water to the ragù – this helps to loosen the mixture and bring all the ingredients together.

Drain the pasta and return it to the pan. Add the sauce and toss everything together with a few freshly chopped basil leaves. Divide among four bowls and serve immediately with a little grated Parmesan.

pizza Enzo
Enzo's pizza

Pizza-making is a boys' job in our house, so three generations of Dallaglio males (Enzo, Vicenzo and me) get stuck in together, generating a snowstorm of flour. This is Enzo's all-time favourite.

Prep time: 30 mins
Cooking time: 8–10 mins for each pizza

SERVES 4

INGREDIENTS

15g fresh yeast
around 200–220ml lukewarm water
450g strong plain flour, plus extra for dusting
1 tsp salt
200ml passata
200g salame piccante
2 balls of mozzarella, sliced
drizzle of olive oil
salt and freshly ground black pepper
a few fresh basil leaves

sacla' tip

Slice some Dallaglio by Sacla' Italian Slow-Baked Tomatoes Marinated With Garlic and scatter over the pizzas before baking.

Preheat the oven to 220°C/200°C fan oven/gas mark 7. Preheat a couple of baking sheets or use a pizza stone if you have one (remember, with one stone, you'll only be able to cook one pizza at a time). To make the dough, put the yeast in a small bowl and add a little of the water. Stir to dissolve the yeast.

Put the flour in a large bowl and stir in the salt. Make a well in the centre and add the yeast liquid and the remaining water. Stir with a knife to bring the ingredients together.

When the mixture starts to look like dough, gather it up from the bowl with your hands and knead it on a floured board for about 10–15 mins until soft, smooth and elastic.

Divide the dough into quarters and tear off four pieces of baking parchment, each roughly 40cm square. Lightly dust with flour. Roll out each piece of dough into a circle on the parchment. This makes it easier to slide them onto the preheated baking sheet, giving you a thin and crispy base.

Spoon over a little passata, then add a few slices of salami and mozzarella. Drizzle with oil, season and slide the paper onto the baking sheets or pizza stone. Bake for 8–10 mins until crisp and golden. Cook the remaining pizzas. Garnish with basil leaves.

nodini al burro e salvia
veal cutlets with butter and sage

I love veal cooked this way. The sage is cooked with the butter, oil and meat and adds real depth of flavour to the finished dish. Make sure you cook the veal thoroughly – there shouldn't be a hint of pink. Pork chops are always an option for this dish, however, if you prefer.

Prep time: 10 mins
Cooking time: 15–20 mins

SERVES 4

INGREDIENTS
4 veal cutlets
salt and freshly ground black pepper
a little vegetable oil
a knob of butter
a few sage leaves
mashed potato and wilted spinach,
    to serve

Season the veal cutlets.

Heat the oil and butter in a large non-stick frying pan. When the butter stops foaming, add the cutlets and cook over a low to medium heat until golden. Turn over and cook the other side.

When the meat is almost cooked, add the sage to the pan, allocating some to each cutlet, and cook for a little longer.

Lift each cutlet onto a plate, garnishing with a drizzle of the herby oil and butter mixture, then spoon on some mashed potato and spinach and serve immediately.

'Veal is very lean and fine-
textured, so be careful
not to let it dry out
when you're cooking it'

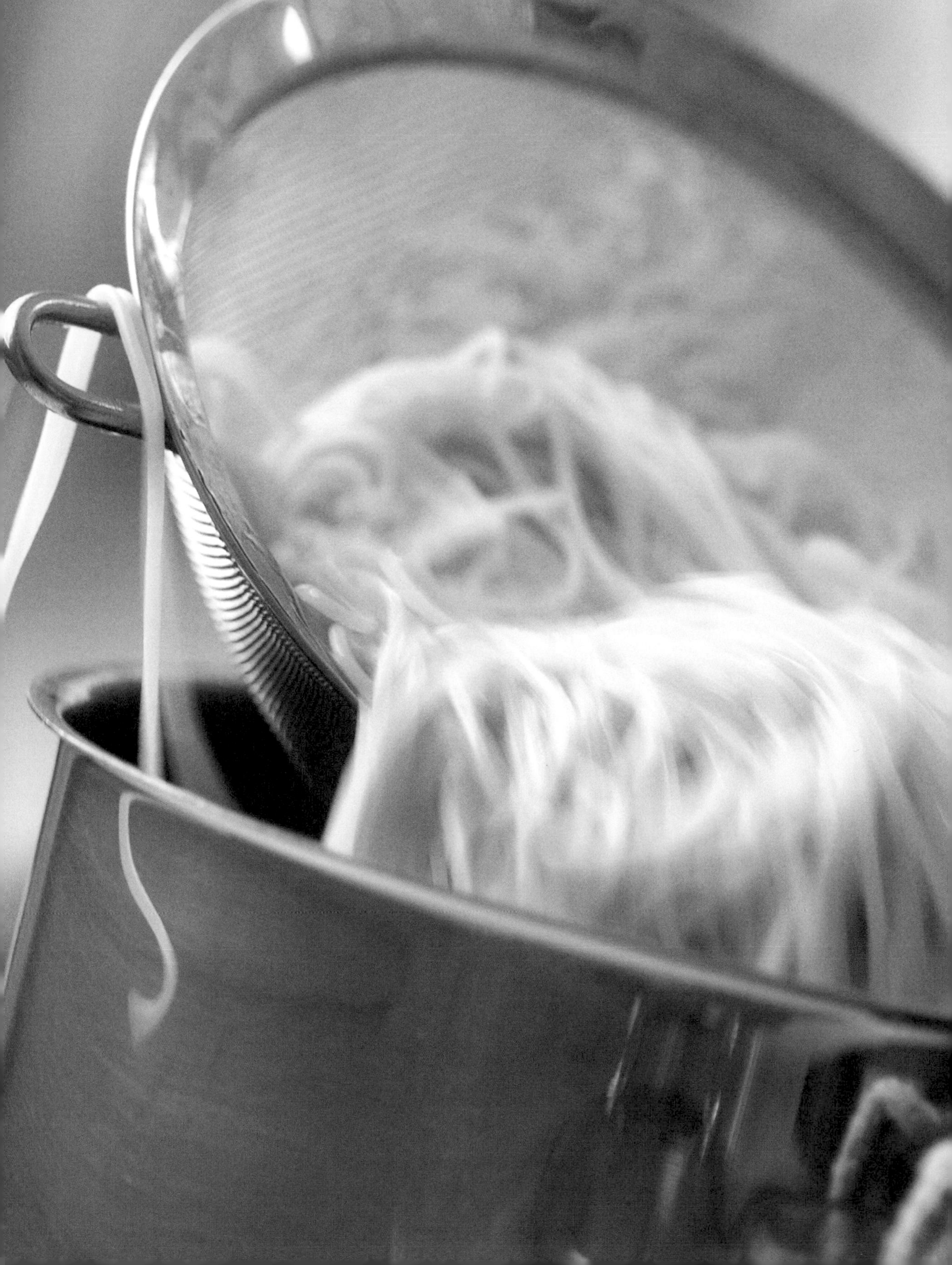

spaghetti con aglio e scampi
spaghetti with prawns and garlic

If you can't get hold of raw prawns, use cooked ones, but add them right at the very end when the oil mixture is in the pan with the pasta to prevent them from overcooking and becoming tough.

Prep time: 5 mins
Cooking time: 15 mins

SERVES 4

INGREDIENTS

400g spaghetti
1 tbsp olive oil
1 fresh chilli, chopped
1 garlic clove, peeled and sliced
300g raw prawns
4 Dallaglio by Sacla' Italian Slow-Baked
   Tomatoes Marinated With Chilli,
   sliced
salt and freshly ground black pepper
2 tbsp freshly chopped parsley

Bring a large pan of salted water to the boil and cook the spaghetti until al dente.

Heat the oil in a pan – a frying pan is good for this recipe – and add the chilli and garlic. Cook gently for about 1 min. Add the prawns and cook for a few minutes until they start to turn pink. Add a splash of cooking water from the pasta at this stage to help them on their way. Stir in the tomatoes and season.

Drain the pasta, then return it to the pan with the prawn mixture and parsley. Toss well and divide among four bowls.

'Fish and liver are brilliant sources of protein, great for repairing wear and tear — I ate loads of it as a rugby player, but kids need to get enough, too'

fegato di vitello alla veneziana
calf's liver with onions

This is one of my father's favourite recipes. It's full of flavour and rich in iron, and needs nothing more than a spoonful of creamy mash and green beans. Ask the butcher to slice the calf's liver for you.

Prep time: 15 mins
Cooking time: 20 mins

SERVES 4

INGREDIENTS

1 tbsp olive oil
1 onion, peeled and finely sliced
15g butter
500g calf's liver, cut into strips
salt and freshly ground black pepper
1 tbsp freshly chopped parsley
mashed potato and steamed green beans,
   to serve

Heat the oil in a pan and fry the onion on a low heat for about 15 mins until softened. Tip onto a plate and set aside.

Add the butter to the pan and allow it to melt, then add the calf's liver and cook over a medium heat, tossing every now and then, until cooked.

Return the onions to the pan with the liver, season well, then add the parsley. Toss everything together and serve immediately with mashed potato and steamed green beans.

pesce al pesto
pesto-topped fish

This is as easy as falling off a log – and it's ready in 20 minutes. Serve it simply with a green salad and boiled new potatoes.

Prep time: 5 mins
Cooking time: around 15 mins

SERVES 4

INGREDIENTS

1½ tbsp olive oil
25g stoned green olives, roughly chopped
3 tbsp Sacla' Classic Basil Pesto
zest of ½ lemon
4 x 125g pieces haddock loin
1 slice bread, whizzed into breadcrumbs
Parmesan cheese
salt and freshly ground black pepper
½ lemon, cut into four wedges

Preheat the oven to 200°C/180°C fan oven/gas mark 6.

Put the oil, olives, pesto and lemon zest in a mini food processor and whiz to make a paste.

Put the fish pieces in an ovenproof dish and top each piece with the pesto mixture. Sprinkle the breadcrumbs evenly over the pesto, and then grate some Parmesan on top.

Season well, then cook in the oven for about 15 mins until the fish is opaque in the middle. Serve with a wedge of lemon to squeeze over.

panzanella
tomato and bread salad

This recipe is ridiculously simple. It's a traditional peasant dish that's perfect for using up a glut of over-ripe tomatoes and bread that's gone stale in the heat of summer. But wait till you taste it – it's bursting with flavour and makes a perfect light lunch in warm weather.

Prep time: 15 mins

SERVES 4

INGREDIENTS

600g ripe tomatoes
1 small red onion, peeled
1 tbsp red wine vinegar
salt and freshly ground black pepper
¼ stale country-style loaf
2–3 tbsp extra virgin olive oil
fresh basil leaves

Halve the tomatoes and use a spoon to scoop out the seeds into a sieve resting over a bowl to catch the juices. Chop the tomatoes roughly and tip into a salad bowl.

Slice the red onion and add to the tomatoes with the red wine vinegar. Season and toss well.

Cut the bread into bite-sized chunks and add to the tomatoes with the olive oil. Toss everything together and add the basil leaves. If you can, cover and set this aside at room temperature for 30 mins to 1 hour before eating. The flavours will mix together and be all the better for it.

cozze alla marinara
fisherman's mussels

This recipe calls for just five ingredients. Mussels have bags of flavour, so they need very little embellishment. My kids use an empty shell to pick the mussels out of the other shells. Serve with plenty of crusty bread to mop up the juices.

Prep time: 20 mins
Cooking time: 5 mins

SERVES 4

INGREDIENTS

1 kg mussels
1 tbsp olive oil
1 garlic clove, peeled and crushed
125ml dry white wine
2 tbsp freshly chopped parsley
crusty bread, to serve

Pick over the mussels and discard any that are broken or remain open when tapped. Rinse well.

Heat the oil in a large pan and gently cook the garlic until just golden. Add the mussels, cover the pan and leave on the hob over a medium heat for a few minutes to steam open.

Add the wine to the pan, cover and bring to the boil. Cook for 1–2 mins.

Sprinkle over the parsley and serve immediately with crusty bread.

'Vincenzo, aged 16, and friends, waiting tables in Valentino Park in Torino in the summer of 1950'

risotto alla milanese
risotto with saffron

This simple and traditional risotto is flavoured with saffron, the world's most expensive spice, and it's one of my all-time favourites.

Prep time: 10 mins
Cooking time: 25 mins

SERVES 4

INGREDIENTS
40g butter
1 tbsp olive oil
1 large onion, peeled and chopped
400g Arborio risotto rice
pinch of saffron
1.4 litres hot vegetable or chicken stock
125ml dry white wine
salt
freshly grated Parmesan cheese

Melt 25g of the butter in a pan over a low heat with the oil. Add the onion and sauté for about 15 mins until softened. Stir in the risotto rice and saffron, and toss around in the mixture for a couple of minutes to coat and heat up the rice.

Pour the hot stock into a pan and bring to a gentle simmer.

Add the white wine and allow it to be absorbed by the rice. Then add the hot stock, one ladleful at a time, allowing each ladleful to be absorbed before adding the next one, stirring constantly. Continue cooking the rice in this way until all the stock is used up and the rice is tender, with a firm bite.

Add the remaining butter, season well and stir in some Parmesan. Divide among four bowls and grate over more cheese if you want.

'Piedmont, where my father, Vincenzo, grew up, has abundant rice harvests — so he takes his risotto very seriously indeed'

frittata di cipolle e piselli
frittata with onions and peas

The omelette is another inventive way that the Italians use up leftovers. Do as they do – raid the fridge and include anything you fancy (even leftover pasta). Whisk the eggs well to get lots of air into them, which makes the mixture light and fluffy.

Prep and cooking time: 20 mins

SERVES 4

INGREDIENTS

200g peas
2 tbsp olive oil
2 large sweet onions, peeled and sliced
6 large eggs
salt and freshly ground black pepper
2 tbsp freshly chopped parsley
salad and crusty bread, to serve

Steam the peas in a pan until just tender and then drain.

Heat the oil in a large non-stick pan and sweat the onions for about 15 mins until soft and just starting to turn golden.

Beat the eggs in a bowl with a whisk and season well. Stir in the parsley. Preheat the grill.

Pour the egg mixture into the pan with the onions, then sprinkle with the peas. Use a wooden spoon to loosen the mixture as it cooks and sticks to the bottom, and allow the uncooked egg to run into the 'holes'. Cook until the egg is almost cooked, then grill until golden. Serve with a salad and crusty bread.

per gli amici di casa

weekend food for friends

These recipes are typical of what we cook at laid-back gatherings of family and friends. Nothing beats getting together around a table for catching up with what matters most – the people you care about.

3

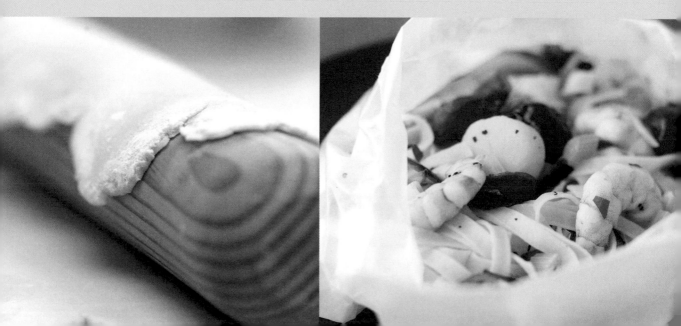

melanzane alla parmigiana
aubergine bake with parmesan

A sumptuous dish that I make when we have vegetarian friends over. The meat-eaters are invariably satisfied, too, as it's so rich. Serve with a green salad and some crusty bread.

Prep time: 25 mins, plus salting time
Cooking time: 40–50 mins

SERVES 4

INGREDIENTS

2 aubergines, sliced to the thickness
  of a £1 coin
3 tbsp olive oil
1 onion, peeled and finely chopped
1 carrot, peeled and finely chopped
1 celery stick, finely chopped
400g can chopped tomatoes
50g freshly grated Parmesan cheese
1–2 balls of mozzarella, thinly sliced
salt and freshly ground black pepper

Place the aubergine slices in a colander and salt each layer. Set aside for 20 mins to extract the bitter juices. Rinse well.

Heat 1 tbsp of the oil in a pan and fry the onion, carrot and celery until softened and just starting to turn golden. Add the chopped tomatoes, with a splash of water to rinse out the can, and bring to the boil. Simmer for 10 mins until it's the consistency of a sauce.

Preheat the oven to 200°C/180°C fan oven/gas mark 6. Meanwhile, fry the aubergines in a pan in the remaining oil until tender on each side.

Take a 1.2-litre ovenproof dish and spoon a little tomato sauce on the base. Layer up the aubergine, Parmesan, tomato sauce and mozzarella, finishing with a layer of mozzarella. Season as you go. Lastly, sprinkle with Parmesan.

Bake in the preheated oven for about 20–30 mins, until bubbling and golden.

sacla' tip

If you're pushed for time, use a 300g jar of Dallaglio by Sacla' Tricolore sauce instead of making the tomato sauce.

abbacchio alla romana
roman-style lamb chops in anchovy and rosemary sauce

This is a classic Roman dish. It's rich and gutsy, so no need for anything more than plain boiled potatoes to go with it, plus, maybe, spinach wilted in butter, or some green beans.

Prep time: 10 mins
Cooking time: 50 mins

SERVES 4

INGREDIENTS

2 tbsp plain flour
salt and freshly ground black pepper
8 lamb cutlets
1 tbsp sunflower oil
2 garlic cloves, peeled and sliced
600ml hot lamb or chicken stock
3 tbsp white wine vinegar
4 anchovies in oil, roughly chopped
2 sprigs of rosemary, roughly chopped

Preheat the oven to 200°C/180°C fan oven/gas mark 6.

Put the flour in a shallow bowl and season well. Dip each lamb cutlet in the seasoned flour to coat.

Heat the oil in a large frying pan. Fry the lamb in batches until golden on each side. Set aside. Add the garlic and remaining flour to the pan and cook for 1–2 mins.

Pour in the hot stock and the vinegar and stir continuously to mix in the flour. Add the anchovies and rosemary and return the cutlets to the pan. Cover and bring to the boil, then transfer to the oven and cook for 30 mins. The sauce will have thickened to a rich gravy and the lamb will be tender.

Try this wine with it...
Luigi d'Alessandro, Cortona Syrah (Tuscany)
Red

scaloppine di pollo alla milanese
milanese chicken breasts

Here's a recipe that my kids can't get enough of. It's basically chicken breasts flattened, then coated in breadcrumbs mixed with thyme and rosemary. You can be generous with the herbs, as that guarantees plenty of flavour. If you want to max the healthiness factor, bake in the oven at 200°C/180°C fan oven/ gas mark 6 for 20 minutes instead of frying. It will come out pale gold and equally delicious. Serve it up with a green salad.

Prep time: 15 mins
Cooking time: 20 mins

SERVES 4

INGREDIENTS

4 skinless chicken breasts
3 tbsp plain flour
2 large eggs, beaten
2 slices white bread, whizzed into
   breadcrumbs
4 sprigs of thyme, freshly chopped
2 sprigs of rosemary, freshly chopped
salt and freshly ground black pepper
a little sunflower oil

Line a chopping board with clingfilm, place two of the chicken breasts on it, then cover with another sheet of clingfilm. Bash them with a rolling pin until they're flattened – ideally they should be about 0.5cm thick. Repeat with the other two breasts.

Put the flour in a shallow bowl, the beaten eggs in another, and the breadcrumbs in yet another. Add the herbs to the breadcrumbs and mix together. Season each bowlful well.

Dip both sides of the flattened chicken breasts in the flour, then in the egg, then finally in the breadcrumbs.

Heat the oil in a large, shallow frying pan and fry the chicken in two batches. Turn down the heat as soon as one side is golden, continue to cook for a few more minutes, then flip over and cook the other side. To check if the chicken is cooked properly, cut right through the middle. The chicken should be completely white with no hint of pink.

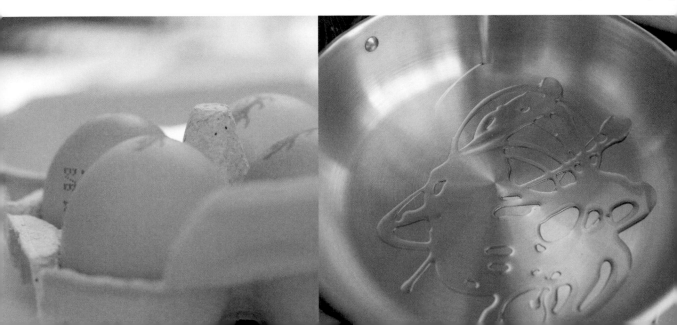

scampi e capesante al cartoccio
prawn and scallop parcels

This dish never fails to get a roar of approval. What I never tell anyone is that it's just about the easiest thing to rustle up in the kitchen.

Prep time: 5 mins
Cooking time: 25 mins

SERVES 4

INGREDIENTS

1 tbsp olive oil, plus extra to drizzle
1 red onion, peeled and finely sliced
½ garlic clove, peeled and crushed
200g cherry tomatoes, halved
½ fennel bulb, chopped, fronds reserved
salt and freshly ground black pepper
400g tagliatelle
200g each scallops and prawns (raw)
1–2 tbsp freshly chopped parsley

Cut four large rectangles of baking parchment about 38 x 50cm each. Preheat the oven to 200°C/180°C fan oven/gas mark 6.

Heat the oil in a pan and fry the onion until softened. Add the garlic and cook for 1 min. Add the cherry tomatoes and the chopped fennel, and cook for 3–4 mins until softened. Season well.

Cook the tagliatelle for 5 mins. Drain well, adding a ladleful of the cooking water to the cherry tomato mixture.

Return the pasta to the pan and add the cherry tomato sauce, season and toss well.

Divide the mixture among the parchment pieces, top each with a quarter of the scallops and prawns. Drizzle over a little oil and sprinkle over the parsley. Fold the parchment into parcels, twisting the ends together so that they stay closed. Put the parcels on a couple of lipped baking sheets and cook in the oven for 20 mins.

Place on plates and serve immediately.

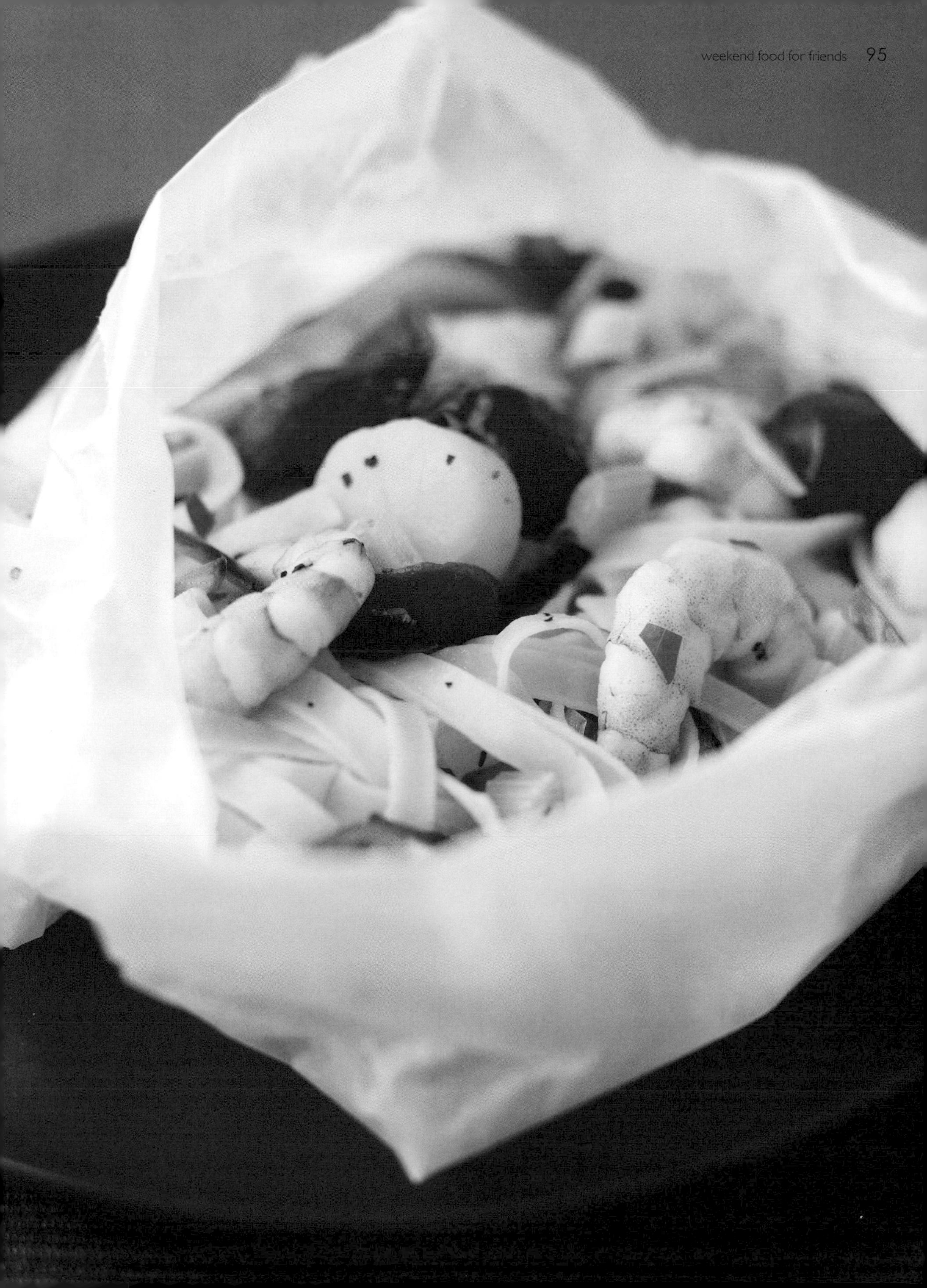

spiedini di pesce
fish kebabs

Simple, quick, eaten in a flash.

Prep time: 10 mins
Cooking time: 5 mins

SERVES 4

INGREDIENTS

4–8 wooden skewers
600g firm white fish, such as pollock,
    cut up into large pieces
2 tbsp mixed herbs, such as oregano
    and thyme
1 garlic clove, peeled and crushed
2 tbsp olive oil
2 tbsp dry white wine
salt and freshly ground black pepper
1–2 lemons, cut into wedges
rocket and tomato salad, to serve

Soak the skewers in cold water for at least an hour.

Pop the fish in a bowl with the herbs, garlic, oil and wine. Season well. Set aside to marinate for 20 mins.

Divide the fish equally among the skewers, finishing with a chunk of lemon, and grill for about 5 mins, turning over halfway through, until the fish is opaque. Serve with the salad.

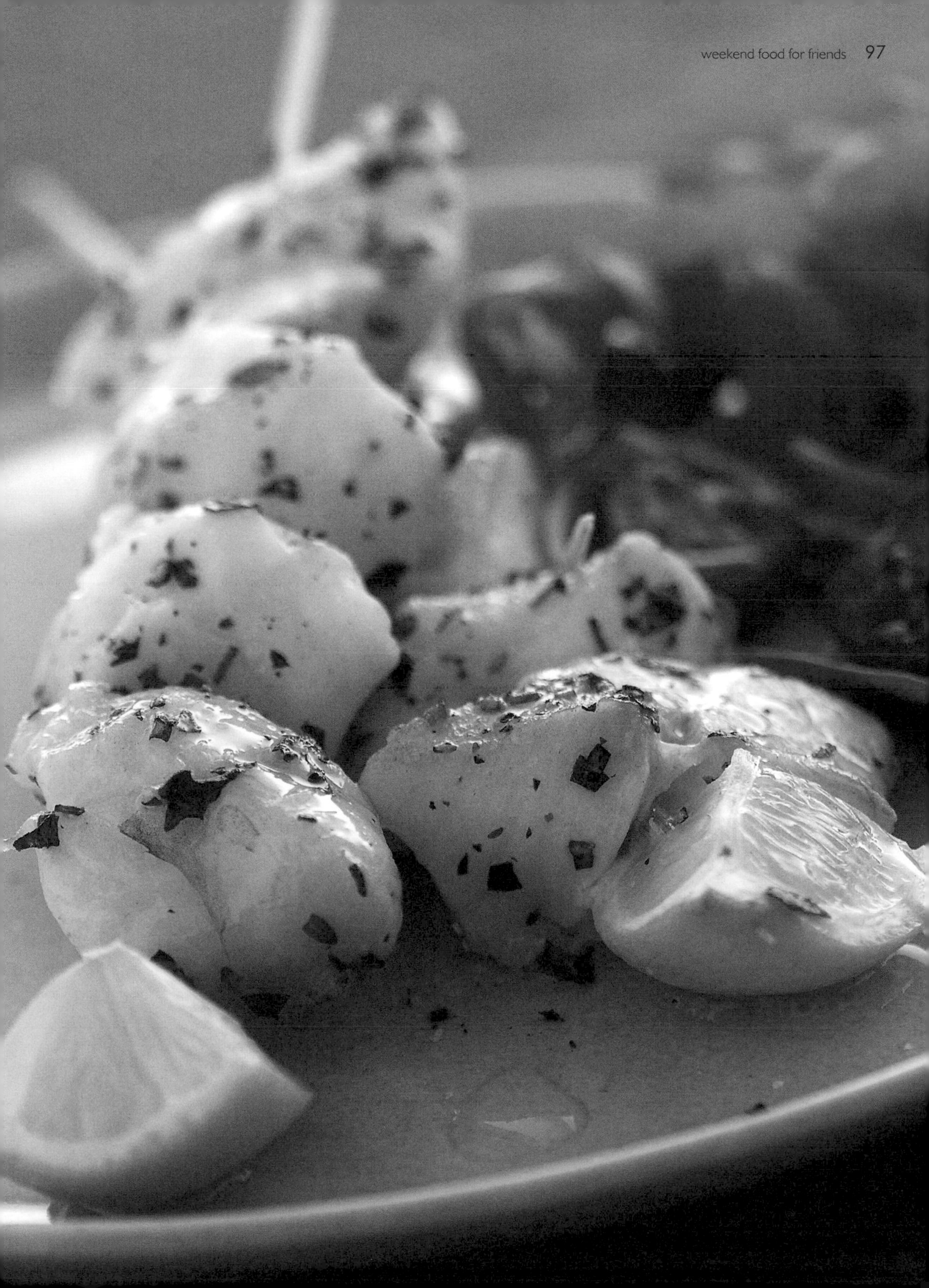

zucca ripiena al forno
baked, stuffed squash

The versatility of this dish makes it useful. If you serve it on its own, it's good for four people, but if you dish it up alongside the Sunday roast, it could stretch to feeding six or eight (or three to four rugby players). I've used thyme for the herb flavouring, but chopped sage or rosemary would work just as well.

Prep time: 15 mins
Cooking time: 45 mins

SERVES 4

INGREDIENTS

2 small pumpkins or squash
olive oil
salt and freshly ground black pepper
1 medium red onion, peeled and
    finely chopped
2 celery sticks, finely chopped
1 red pepper, finely chopped
a few sprigs of thyme
125g long-grain rice
400ml hot vegetable stock
70g pancetta, cut into cubes
1–2 tbsp freshly chopped parsley
green salad, to serve

Preheat the oven to 200°C/180°C fan/gas mark 6.

Halve the pumpkin or squash lengthways, scoop out the seeds and discard. Put in a shallow roasting tin and drizzle with a little oil. Season and roast for 30–40 mins until just tender.

Heat 1 tbsp olive oil in a pan and fry the onion, celery, red pepper and thyme until softened and golden. Stir in the rice and season, then add the hot stock and cover with a lid. Turn the heat down to low and cook according to the timings on the pack.

Meanwhile, in a separate pan, dry fry the pancetta until golden. Drain well.

When the rice is cooked, stir the pancetta and parsley through it. Remove the pumpkin from the oven, fill with the rice mixture, then return to the oven for 5 mins to warm through. Serve immediately with a green salad.

'Italian food is all about using seasonal ingredients — whatever's fresh at the market that day'

pesce in crosta
fish pie

I love this recipe because you can chuck in whatever fish takes your fancy. Sometimes I mix up white and smoked fish, sometimes I keep it very simple and stick to white fish only. To make it a bit posher, I use salmon and prawns, as I've done here. You can also make the sauce with stock instead of milk, which gives it a slightly lighter feel.

Prep time: 30 mins
Cooking time: about 1 hour

SERVES 4

INGREDIENTS
15g butter
2 shallots, peeled and finely chopped
1 small fennel bulb, chopped
salt and freshly ground black pepper
a splash of vermouth
1 tbsp plain flour
450ml hot fish or vegetable stock
600g mixed fish, such as salmon, halibut
   and prawns
200g frozen peas, thawed
2 tbsp freshly chopped parsley
750g potatoes, sliced to the thickness
   of a £1 coin
2 slices white bread, whizzed into
   breadcrumbs
15g pecorino cheese, freshly grated

Preheat the oven to 200°C/180°C fan oven/gas mark 6.

Melt the butter in a pan and gently fry the shallots and fennel until soft. Season well. Add the vermouth and simmer until the liquid is absorbed by the vegetables.

Stir in the flour and cook for 1 min, then slowly add the hot stock and carry on stirring until all the stock is incorporated into the sauce.

Put the fish and peas into a 1.2-litre ovenproof dish. Stir the parsley into the sauce and season well. Pour the sauce over the fish.

Top with the potatoes, then sprinkle with the breadcrumbs and pecorino. Bake in the oven for 45–50 mins until bubbling and golden and the potatoes are tender. Test them by pushing the point of a sharp knife into them.

Try this wine with it...
Cantine di Monteforte, Pinot Grigio/Chardonnay (Veneto)
White

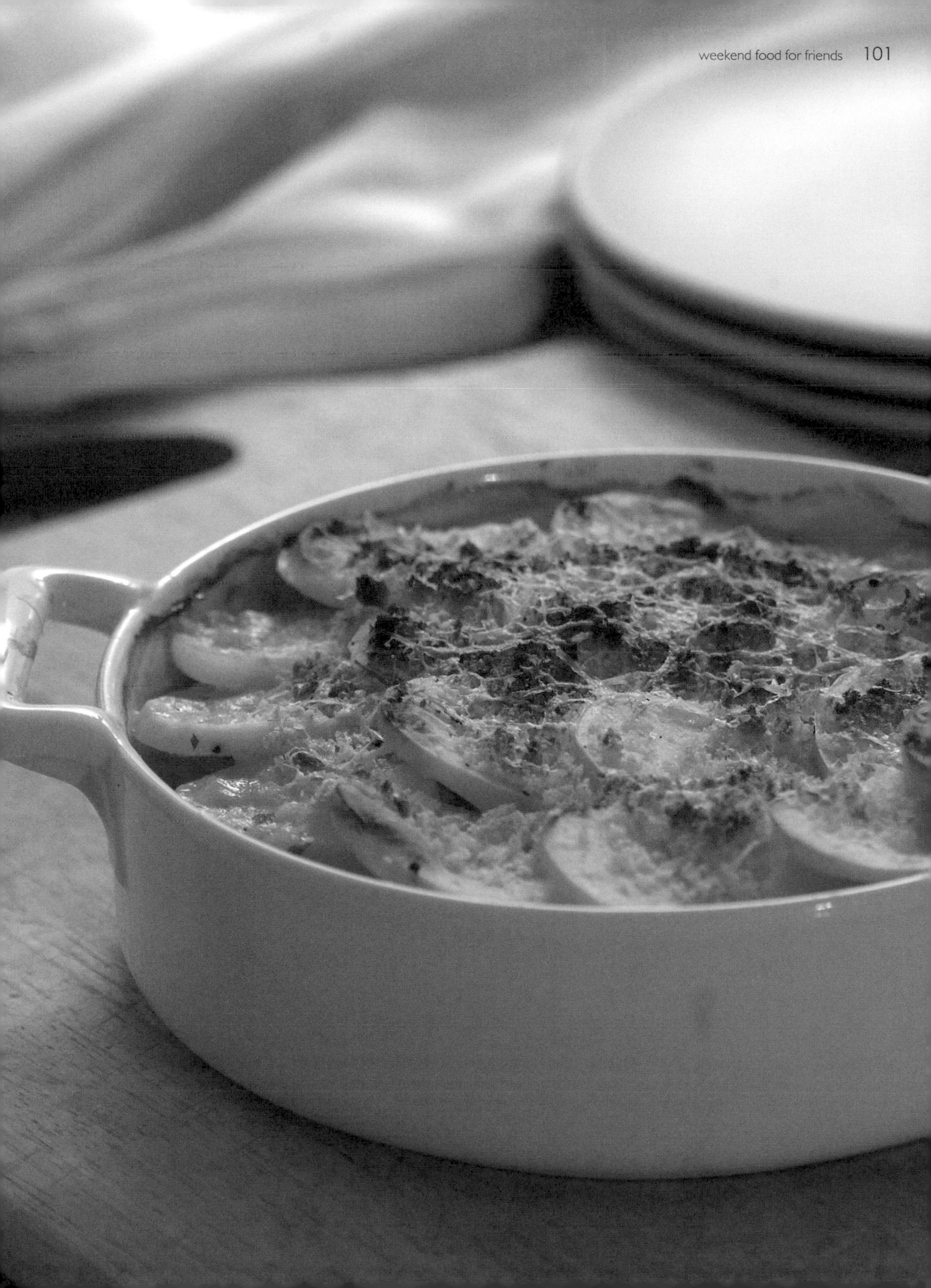

fagioli all'uccelletto
beans in tomato sauce

Here's our Italian version of baked beans. You need to soak the beans the day before, but that's not a hassle. It's a simple dish to make and it's healthy, student-style grub that everyone loves: cheap, easy and tasty. It'll also keep well in the fridge for three or four days.

Prep time: 10 mins, plus at least 8 hours soaking

Cooking time: 1 hour 10 mins

SERVES 4

INGREDIENTS

125g dried cannellini or borlotti beans
1 onion, peeled and chopped
1 bay leaf
1 sprig of rosemary
1 tbsp olive oil
1 celery stick, chopped
1 carrot, peeled and chopped
200g can chopped tomatoes
1 vegetable stock cube
salt and freshly ground black pepper
crusty bread and Sacla' Fiery Chilli Pesto, to serve

Put the beans in a sealable container and cover with plenty of cold water. Cover with the lid and leave to soak for at least 8 hours.

Drain and rinse the beans, then put them in a pan with the onion, bay leaf and sprig of rosemary. Add 1 litre of cold water and cover. Bring to the boil, reduce the heat, then simmer gently for 1 hour.

When the beans are cooked, heat the oil in a saucepan and sauté the celery and carrot for about 10 mins. Drain the beans and onions, discarding the bay leaf and rosemary sprig, but reserving the cooking liquid, and add the bean mixture to the pan with the celery and carrot. Stir everything together.

Add 200ml of the cooking liquid, the chopped tomatoes and the vegetable stock cube. Stir to dissolve the cube. Season and simmer for about 10 mins until thick and saucy. Serve immediately with bread and the chilli pesto.

Try this wine with it...
Cantine Leonardo da Vinci, Chianti (Tuscany)
Red

linguine alla carbonara
linguine with ham, eggs and cheese

Some people think that cream is essential for this sauce, but it's not. The secret is to cook the pancetta in oil, so there's enough fat in the pan to coat the pasta and mix with the eggy sauce. The amount of Parmesan you add is up to you, so I always put an extra chunk on the table in case anyone wants more. If you can't get hold of pancetta, use streaky bacon instead.

Prep time: 5 mins
Cooking time: 10–15 mins

SERVES 4

INGREDIENTS

400g linguine
2 tbsp olive oil
150g pancetta, cut into small cubes
4 medium eggs
25g freshly grated Parmesan cheese,
   plus extra to serve
salt and freshly ground black pepper

Bring a large pan of salted water to the boil and cook the linguine until al dente.

Heat the oil in a pan and fry the pancetta until golden. In a bowl, whisk the eggs and Parmesan until creamy. Season well.

Drain the pasta and return it to the pan. Add the pancetta plus any oil, and immediately pour in the egg mixture. Stir everything together. Divide among four bowls and serve immediately with lots of freshly ground black pepper and extra Parmesan.

crespoline al prosciutto e ricotta
pancakes with ham and ricotta

These savoury pancakes are a great way of tarting up leftover ingredients.
I've used ricotta and ham, but if there are any leftover cooked vegetables
in the fridge, bung them in, too.

Prep time: 10 mins
Cooking time: 30 mins

SERVES 4 (2 pancakes per person)

INGREDIENTS
425ml milk
125g plain flour
2 medium eggs
salt and freshly ground black pepper
a little sunflower oil, for frying
500g ricotta cheese
200g ham, chopped
2 tbsp freshly chopped basil
butter, for greasing
300g jar Dallaglio by Sacla'
    Bolognese sauce
freshly grated Parmesan cheese

Put the milk and flour in a bowl and whisk together. Whisk in the
eggs and season. Set aside for 20 mins.

Heat the oil in a medium frying pan and ladle in a spoonful of
the batter – I'm going to be specific here: you need around
80ml batter per pancake, making a total of eight. Swirl the batter
around the pan to cover the base and cook over a medium heat
for 2–3 mins until golden. Flip the pancake over and cook the
other side. Slide onto a plate and transfer to a warm oven. Repeat
until all the batter has been used.

Preheat the oven to 210°C/190°C fan oven/gas mark 6/7.

Mix together the ricotta, ham and basil in a bowl, seasoning well.
Divide equally among the pancakes and fold up.

Place the pancakes side by side in a 1.2-litre ovenproof dish
greased with butter. Pour the Dallaglio bolognese sauce into a
bowl and stir in 50–100ml water to loosen it. Spoon the sauce
over the pancakes and sprinkle with grated Parmesan. Bake in the
preheated oven for 15–20 mins until heated through.

minestrone del nonno
grandpa's vegetable soup

This time-honoured Italian soup uses whatever vegetables are in season. Start it a day ahead, as the borlotti beans need to be soaked in cold water. My father's finishing touch is crushed garlic mixed with parsley, added at the end.

Prep time: 15 mins, plus overnight
    soaking
Cooking time: 1 hour 40 mins

SERVES 4

INGREDIENTS
150g dried borlotti beans
1 tbsp olive oil
1 onion, peeled and chopped
1 celery stick, chopped
1 carrot, peeled and chopped
1.2 litres hot vegetable stock
1 potato, peeled and diced
200g can chopped tomatoes
100g green beans, chopped
1 courgette, chopped
100g peas
salt and freshly ground black pepper
50g capelli d'angelo (angel hair
    spaghetti), broken into pieces
1 garlic clove, peeled
2 tbsp freshly chopped parsley
freshly grated Parmesan cheese, to serve

Put the beans in a large sealable container and cover with double the volume of water. Cover with the lid and leave to soak overnight.

The next day, heat the oil in a pan and fry the onion, celery and carrot for about 5 mins until just softening.

Drain the borlotti beans, discard the water and add the beans to the pan with the hot stock. Cover, bring to the boil, then turn the heat down low and simmer for about 1 hour.

Add the diced potato and cook for a further 30 mins. Add the tomatoes, green beans, courgette and peas and season well. Cook for 5 mins.

Add the pasta and cook for about 4 mins. Meanwhile, chop the garlic and the parsley together and season with a little salt.

Divide the soup between the bowls, then stir in the garlic and parsley mix, and add a little grated Parmesan.

Sacla' tip

In place of the garlic and parsley mix, add a dollop of Sacla' Classic Basil Pesto to the minestrone to serve.

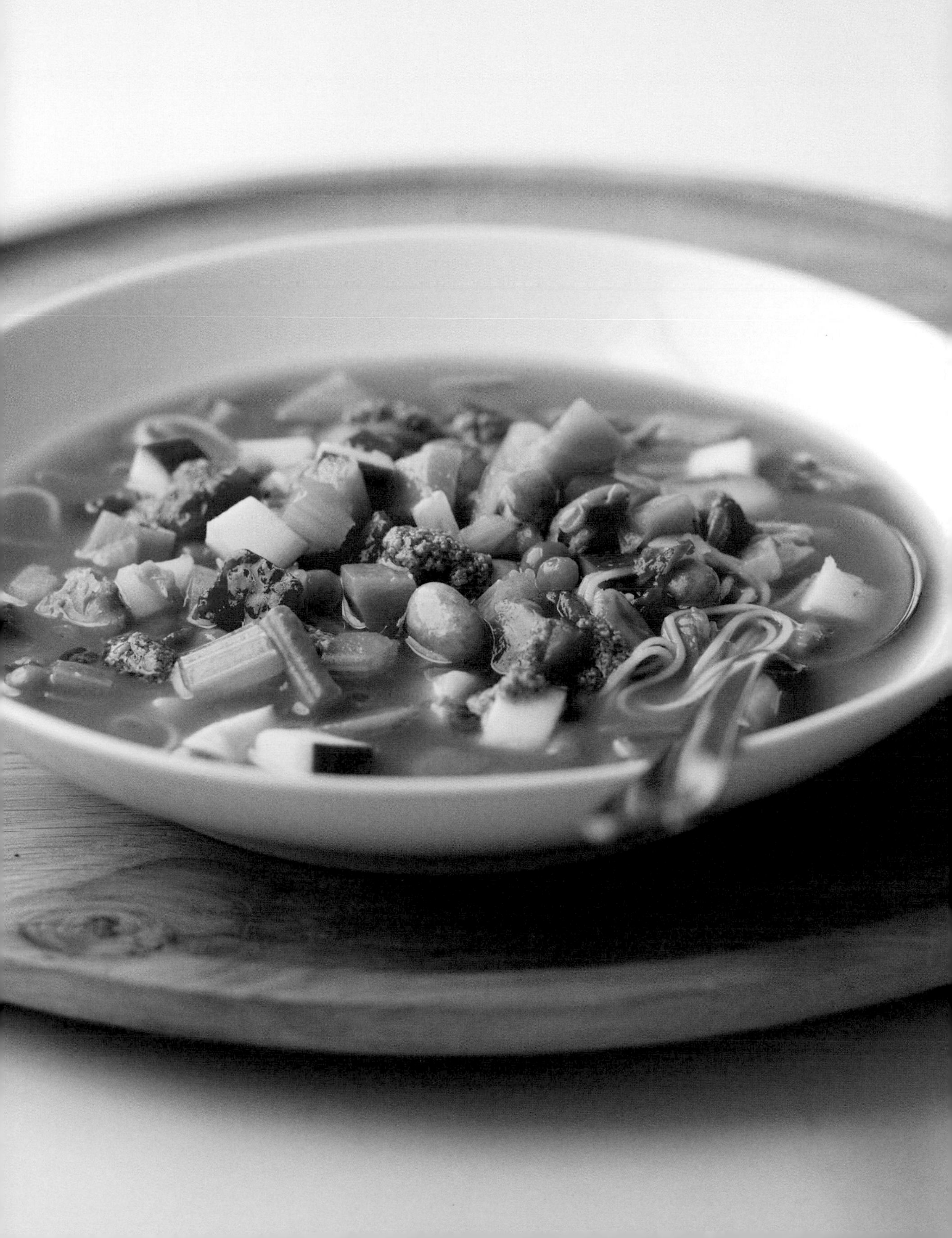

spezzatino di pollo
chicken stew with lemon

Chicken thighs suit this dish better than any other part of the bird – they have an earthier flavour than chicken breasts, so they work well with the garlic and lemon. Serve with tagliatelle or your choice of vegetables.

Prep time: 20 mins
Cooking time: 40 mins

SERVES 4

INGREDIENTS

2 tbsp olive oil
1 onion, peeled and roughly chopped
1 tbsp plain flour
salt and freshly ground black pepper
6 skinless, boneless chicken thighs,
    chopped
8 garlic cloves, peeled
½ lemon, chopped
500ml hot chicken stock
2 tbsp freshly chopped parsley

Preheat the oven to 200°C/180°C fan oven/gas mark 6.

Heat the oil in a large, flat sauté pan with lid and cook the onion very gently for about 5 mins.

Put the flour in a shallow dish, season it, then toss the chicken thighs in it. Cook the chicken in batches in the sauté pan with the onion until golden on all sides – it doesn't need to cook through completely.

Tip any remaining seasoned flour into the pan and return the chicken to the pan, along with the garlic cloves and chopped lemon. Pour in the hot stock, cover and bring to the boil. Transfer to the preheated oven and cook for 30 mins until the chicken is tender and the garlic soft. Stir in the parsley and serve.

Try this wine with it...
Midolini, Rosacroce Chardonnay (Friuli Venezia Giulia)
White

lasagne di verdure
vegetable lasagne

The squash family of vegetables make good companion ingredients – cooking enhances their sweetness, but also the flavours of other ingredients that are paired with them. This is good eaten cold the next day, too.

Prep time: 20 mins
Cooking time: 45 mins

SERVES 4–6

INGREDIENTS

15g butter
500g spinach, washed
salt and freshly ground black pepper
nutmeg, for grating
1 tbsp olive oil
1 small onion, peeled and finely chopped
1 red pepper, deseeded and chopped
450g pumpkin or squash, chopped
300g jar Dallaglio by Sacla' Tricolore sauce
a few sprigs of basil leaves, roughly chopped
about 6 dried lasagne sheets
50g mozzarella, chopped
25g freshly grated Parmesan cheese

Preheat the oven to 200°C/180°C fan oven/gas mark 6.

Melt the butter in a very large pan and add the spinach. Cook for a couple of minutes until it wilts down. You might need to do this in two batches. Season with salt and pepper and a little nutmeg.

Heat the oil in a pan and sauté the onion, pepper and pumpkin or squash for about 15 mins, covered with a lid, until softened. The steam will help to cook the vegetables. By the end of this stage, you'll notice that the pumpkin is quite soft and squashy.

Set aside 100g Dallaglio by Sacla' Tricolore sauce, then add the rest to the pan with the basil. Fill the empty jar with cold water and add to the pan. Bring to the boil and bubble for 5 mins until thickened and saucy.

Line a 1.2-litre dish with lasagne sheets, then spoon over a third of the spinach. Cover with a third of the vegetable sauce. Repeat until all the ingredients are used up, then spoon the reserved sauce over the last layer of lasagne. Cover with the mozzarella and sprinkle over the Parmesan.

Cook in the oven for 25 mins until the lasagne is tender and the top is golden and bubbling.

zucchine ripieni
stuffed courgettes

If you want to make the most of courgettes, this is the way to do it. By the way, a quick word about shallots: I've used them in quite a few of the recipes in this book, including this one. That's because they're milder than onions, they have a slightly sweeter flavour, and they also take less time to cook, which is always a good enough reason in our house.

Prep time: 15 mins
Cooking time: 35 mins

SERVES 4

INGREDIENTS

1 tbsp olive oil
4 large shallots, peeled and finely chopped
6 small–medium courgettes,
   halved lengthways
salt and freshly ground black pepper
50g pine nuts
1 tsp thyme leaves
a few sprigs of mint
200ml hot vegetable stock
50g breadcrumbs
25–50g pecorino cheese, grated

Preheat the oven to 200°C/180°C fan oven/gas mark 6.

Heat the oil in a pan and fry the shallots until softened. Using a teaspoon, run down the length of the halved courgettes to hollow them out. Roughly chop these bits and add to the shallots with a drizzle more oil if needed. Season well.

Add the pine nuts to the pan with the thyme and cook for 5–10 mins until softened. Stir in the mint.

Put the halved courgettes in a large ovenproof dish, hollowed-out-side up. Season well, then spoon the cooked mixture down the length of each one. Pour in the hot stock.

Sprinkle with the breadcrumbs and cheese, and cover the dish with foil. Cook in the preheated oven for 20 mins, then uncover and cook for a further 10 mins to brown the top.

Try this wine with it...
Planeta, Cerasuolo di Vittoria (Sicily)
Red

tonno con salsa di pomodoro
tuna with tomato and white wine sauce

As a guy who likes to look after himself, fish is a big favourite of mine. It's a good source of lean protein and vitamin B, and it packs a powerful punch of brain-boosting omega 3. And whether you fry, grill or poach it, it takes less than 30 minutes from pan to plate.

Prep time: 5 mins
Cooking time: 20 mins

SERVES 4

INGREDIENTS

1 tbsp olive oil
1 onion, peeled and finely chopped
2 celery sticks, sliced
100ml white wine
150ml hot fish stock
200g can chopped tomatoes
1 bay leaf
50g pitted black olives
salt and freshly ground black pepper
4 x 150g yellowfin tuna steaks
rocket, to serve

Heat the oil in a wide shallow pan and cook the onion and celery until softened and starting to turn golden.

Add the wine, hot stock, tomatoes and bay leaf, and bring to the boil. Stir in the olives and season. Simmer, covered, for 10 mins.

Lower the tuna steaks into the sauce and cook for about 10 mins – the fish will turn opaque when it's done. Take out the bay leaf, and serve with rocket.

sacla' tip

As an alternative to the tomatoes, bay leaf and black olives, use Sacla' Italian Tomato & Olive Big Bold Italian sauce.

tiella barese
potato and mushroom cheese bake

Here's a heart-warming dish that needs no more than a green salad to go with it. Onions, softened until golden, are stirred together with potatoes and mushrooms, and covered with breadcrumbs and cheese.

Prep time: 10 mins
Cooking time: 40 mins

SERVES 4

INGREDIENTS

1 kg potatoes
2 tbsp olive oil, plus extra for drizzling
1 onion, peeled and sliced
200g chestnut mushrooms, sliced
400ml hot vegetable stock
salt and freshly ground black pepper
2 tbsp freshly chopped thyme
2 tbsp breadcrumbs
2 tbsp freshly grated Parmesan cheese

Peel the potatoes and cut them in half. Put them in a large pan of cold salted water and simmer for 10 mins. Drain and slice into 0.5cm rounds.

Preheat the oven to 180°C/160°C fan/gas mark 4.

Heat the oil in an ovenproof sauté pan and fry the onion until softened. Add the mushrooms and continue to cook until golden.

Slide the potatoes into the pan and toss everything together. Pour over the hot stock, season, and sprinkle with the thyme, breadcrumbs and Parmesan. Drizzle with a little more oil, then cook in the preheated oven for about 30–40 mins until the potatoes are cooked.

'The 1987 Ampleforth 7s team. I'm top left — in those days I played on the wing!'

'It's a dish in itself, but it'll feed a crowd if you serve it with meat or fish'

crema di zucca
butternut squash soup

This silky smooth soup tastes wickedly rich and is really easy to make. When I remember, I double the quantity and freeze half so that there's always some handy for when we're pushed for time.

Prep time: 20 mins
Cooking time: 45 mins

SERVES 4–6

INGREDIENTS

1 tbsp olive oil
1 onion, peeled and finely chopped
1 carrot, peeled and finely chopped
1 celery stick, finely chopped
1 garlic clove, peeled and crushed
1 small butternut squash, peeled and diced
salt and freshly ground black pepper
1 litre hot vegetable stock
1 bay leaf
freshly grated Parmesan cheese

Heat the oil in a pan and add the onion, carrot and celery. Cover and cook over a low heat for 10–15 mins until softened.

Add the garlic and squash, and cook for a few minutes in the softened vegetables. Season well.

Add the hot stock and bay leaf to the pan, season and cover. Bring to the boil, then turn the heat down to a simmer and cook for 20–30 mins until the squash is soft and tender.

Remove and discard the bay leaf. Pour into a blender or food processor and whiz until smooth. Return to the pan, check the seasoning and reheat gently. You may need to add a little more water if the soup is too thick.

Ladle into bowls and grate over a little Parmesan.

Sacla' tip
Serve with a generous dollop of Sacla' Classic Basil Pesto.

arancini
risotto balls

Nothing is wasted in the Italian kitchen, so if my grandmother ever had any risotto left over, the next day she'd make it into balls and serve it to us for breakfast. This recipe is a little more refined – when you bite into one, there's a piece of melted mozzarella hidden inside. They're rich, so serve with a rocket salad.

Prep time: 20 mins
Cooking time: 15 mins

SERVES 4

INGREDIENTS
a little orange zest
half the leftover *risotto primavera*
    (see page 66)
a little orange zest
50g mozzarella, roughly chopped
a little plain flour
1 medium egg
salt
5 slices of white bread, whizzed
    into breadcrumbs
sunflower oil, for frying

Mix the orange zest into the risotto. Using a dessert spoon, take spoonfuls of the mixture and push your thumb into the middle to make a small hole. Fill with a piece of mozzarella, then wrap the rest of the risotto around the mozzarella. Continue until you've made all the balls – there should be about 16.

Put the flour in a bowl, beat the egg in another and season, then tip the breadcrumbs into a third bowl.

Coat the risotto balls first in the flour, then toss in the egg, and finally coat with the breadcrumbs.

Pour about 5cm oil into a shallow pan, then fry the balls in batches over a medium heat, until golden all over. Sprinkle with salt before serving.

Try this wine with it...
Cusumano, Nero d'Avola (Sicily)
Red

'Bite into one and you get a delicious surprise of melted mozzarella inside'

pasta con salsiccia
penne with sausage, lemon and cream

It's funny how two or three sausages just slip down, one after the other, but for this recipe even I find that you only need one sausage per person. Choose a good herby banger to give a full and rounded flavour.

Prep time: 20 mins
Cooking time: 30 mins

SERVES 4

INGREDIENTS

1 tbsp olive oil
2 large shallots, peeled and chopped
½ fennel bulb, chopped
1 celery stick, chopped
½ tsp fennel seeds, crushed
4 good-quality sausages
zest of ½ lemon
salt and freshly ground black pepper
50ml double cream
150ml hot chicken or vegetable stock
400g penne
1 tbsp freshly chopped parsley

Bring a large pan of salted water to the boil.

Heat the oil in a pan and sauté the shallots, chopped fennel and celery over a low to medium heat for about 10 mins, until the vegetables start to caramelise.

Stir in the fennel seeds and cook for about 1–2 mins. Slit the skins of the sausages and add the sausagemeat to the pan with the lemon zest. Season well. Use a wooden spoon to break down the meat while it browns.

Pour in the cream and hot stock, then cover and bring to the boil. By this stage, the sausagemeat should have broken down and the mixture should look more like the consistency of a sauce. Simmer for 10–15 mins.

While the sauce is simmering, cook the penne until al dente. Add a ladleful of the cooking water to the sausage sauce, then drain the pasta well. Return the penne to the pan, pour in the sausage sauce, add the chopped parsley and toss everything together. Serve immediately.

calzone
ham and spinach pizza pockets

Calzone means 'trouser leg' in Italian. I'm not sure of the link with pizza dough folded over to look like a Cornish pasty, but nevertheless, the Italians call it *calzone!* I keep the filling simple: Dallaglio Napoletana sauce, spinach and a slice of ham.

Prep time: 30 mins
Cooking time: 15–20 mins

SERVES 4

INGREDIENTS
a little olive oil, for greasing and brushing
1 quantity of pizza dough (see page 72)
a little plain flour, for dusting
300g jar Dallaglio by Sacla' Napoletana
  sauce
100g spinach
4 slices ham
salt and freshly ground black pepper

Preheat the oven to 200°C/180°C fan oven/gas mark 6.

Grease two baking sheets with a little oil. Divide the dough into quarters and roll out one piece into a 22cm round, as if you're making a pizza.

Spread about 1–2 tbsp of the Napoletana sauce over one half of the dough, top with a quarter of the spinach and a piece of ham, and season. Fold the other half on top and curl the edges of the dough round as if you're making a Cornish pasty. Brush with oil and place on the prepared baking sheet. Repeat with the remaining dough and ingredients.

Bake in the oven for 15–20 mins until golden. Warm the remaining sauce in a pan. Put a calzone on each plate, then spoon a little of the warmed sauce over each.

Try this wine with it...
A Mano, Rosato (Puglia)
Rosé

torta rustica
mozzarella, leek and ham pie

As the name suggests, this literally translates as 'rustic tart' – which means you can put whatever you like in it. Don't use too many watery vegetables, though, otherwise the base of the pastry will turn into a soggy mess. You need to bake this pie on a high temperature to start off with, then reduce the heat and cook for a little longer so that the pastry cooks right through.

Prep time: 30 mins
Cooking time: 1 hour 5 mins

SERVES 4

INGREDIENTS
15g butter
2 large leeks, finely chopped
salt and freshly ground black pepper
500g ready-made shortcrust pastry
a little plain flour, for dusting
1 plum tomato, sliced
125g mozzarella
100g ham, roughly chopped
1 medium egg, beaten

Melt the butter in a pan and fry the leeks gently until softened and starting to turn golden. Season well. Transfer into a sieve resting over a bowl to cool.

Preheat the oven to 230°C/210°C fan oven/gas mark 8.

Roll out two-thirds of the pastry on a clean work surface lightly dusted with flour, and line a 20cm round tin with the pastry. Spoon the leeks over the base, top with the tomato slices, mozzarella and ham. Season well.

Roll out the remaining pastry and use it to make a lid. Place it on top, tucking it under the edges of the pastry that forms the bottom of the pie. Fold the edges of the pastry forming the pie bottom over the lid and press down. Prick the lid all over. Brush with the beaten egg and bake in the oven for 20 mins, then reduce the temperature to 170°C/150°C fan oven/gas mark 3 for 35 mins until golden all over.

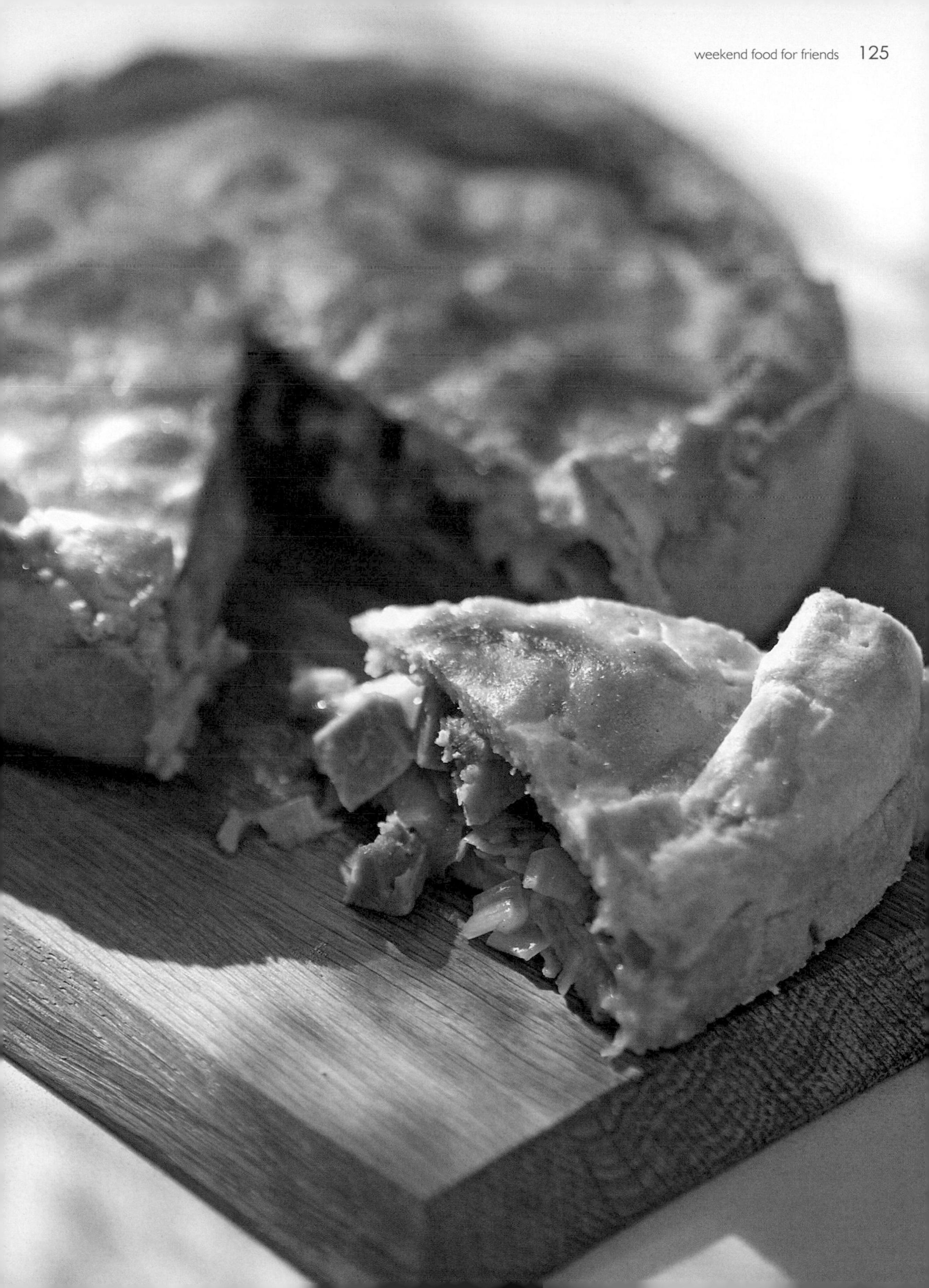

piatti per occasioni speciali
special occasions

4

Italian food is rarely fussy, but these recipes are for when
we want to mark an event by pushing the boat out
a little more than usual. Often my kids muck in,
and that's when I'm at my most contented.

brasato al barolo
braised beef in barolo

Barolo, the red wine used in this dish, comes from my family's Piedmont region. It's big, powerful and gutsy and is one of my favourite Italian wines. Serve the broth in which it's cooked just as it is with the vegetables, or make into a smooth gravy, as I've suggested here.

Prep time: 20 mins
Cooking time: about 2 hours

SERVES 4

INGREDIENTS
1 tbsp olive oil
1 medium onion, peeled and
    finely chopped
2 celery sticks, finely chopped
2 small carrots, peeled and finely chopped
1 garlic clove, peeled and chopped
1 kg topside of beef
salt and freshly ground black pepper
400ml Barolo wine
bouquet garni (a bay leaf, a few parsley
    stalks, a few sprigs of thyme)
15g butter
1 tbsp plain flour
potatoes and steamed green beans,
    to serve

Heat the oil in a pan, add the onion, celery and carrots and gently cook for 5–10 mins. Add the garlic and cook for 1 min.

Season the beef, then add it to the pan, turning it around until browned and done all over. Add the wine and bouquet garni, cover and bring to a simmer. Cook gently for about 1½–2 hours until tender.

Remove the beef from the pan and set aside on a warmed plate. In a separate pan, melt the butter and stir in the flour. Cook for 1–2 mins until the mixture starts to bubble and has the consistency of a paste. Take the bouquet garni out of the sauce and gradually pour the sauce into the pan with the butter/flour paste, whisking all the time as you go. Bring to the boil and simmer for 5 mins until thickened.

Put a stick blender into the pan and whiz until smooth. Keep warm while you slice the beef. Serve with fried, sliced potatoes and steamed green beans.

Try this wine with it...
Oddero, Barolo (Piedmont)
Red

lasagne con ricotta e castagne
chestnut and ricotta lasagne

There are other recipes in this book that call for ready-made lasagne sheets, but here I've included a recipe for fresh lasagne. It takes me back to summer holidays with my grandparents in Italy, where making the pasta involved the whole family – happy days. It's worth having a go if you have a pasta machine, as it's really not difficult. One shortcut that you might want to try, though, is whizzing the chestnuts in a food processor.

Prep time: 50 mins, plus resting time for the pasta
Cooking time: 30 mins

SERVES 4

INGREDIENTS
200g 00 pasta flour
2 large eggs
1 tsp oil
3 shallots, peeled and finely chopped
250g ricotta
250g mascarpone
200g whole chestnuts, finely chopped
1 tbsp each freshly chopped parsley and thyme
salt and freshly ground black pepper
nutmeg, for grating
butter, for greasing
25g freshly grated Parmesan cheese

Sift the flour onto a clean board or work surface and crack the eggs into the centre. Use a fork or your (well-scrubbed) fingers to mix together the egg and slowly draw in the flour.

Continue to work the flour in until you make a dough. Knead briefly until soft and sticky. Cover with clingfilm and leave to rest for 20 mins.

Heat the oil in a small pan and fry the shallots gently until softened. Tip into a bowl and allow to cool. When cooled, add the ricotta, mascarpone, chestnuts and herbs, and season well with salt, freshly ground black pepper and a little nutmeg.

Divide the pasta into thirds and roll out each portion thinly, using a pasta machine. Trim to make rectangles to fit a 1.2-litre ovenproof dish.

Preheat the oven to 200°C/180°C fan oven/gas mark 6.

Cook the pasta in boiling salted water for a few minutes, then drain and lay on baking parchment briefly.

Butter the dish, then layer up the pasta and filling alternately, finishing with a layer of pasta. Sprinkle the Parmesan over the top. Bake in the preheated oven for 25 mins until golden and hot all the way through.

porchetta alla romana
roast pork stuffed with herbs

You need loin of pork, not tenderloin, for this recipe. Make sure the meat has a generous covering of skin so there's enough crackling to go round. If you buy it the day before you cook it, take it out of its wrapping and put it in a dish. Dab it all over with a kitchen towel to mop up any moisture from the skin, and put it in the fridge overnight. This helps to make really crisp crackling. Take the meat out about 30 minutes before roasting.

Prep time: 15 mins
Cooking time: about 2 hours

SERVES 4

INGREDIENTS

1 tbsp olive oil
2 shallots, peeled and finely chopped
1 garlic clove, peeled and crushed
1 sprig of rosemary, finely chopped
20g parsley, chopped
a few sprigs of thyme
2 Dallaglio by Sacla' Slow-Baked
    Tomatoes Marinated With Garlic,
    roughly chopped
1.3 kg pork loin, skin scored
salt and freshly ground black pepper

Preheat the oven to its highest setting.

Heat the oil in a pan and fry the shallots for about 10 mins until softened. Stir in the garlic and cook for 1–2 mins.

Tip into a mini food processor and add the herbs and tomatoes. Whiz to make a paste.

Open out the pork and season well. Cut diagonally along the flesh of the pork to make a pocket. Spread the paste inside, then wrap up the pork and tie it with string. Transfer to a roasting tin and rub salt all over the skin. Pour a glass of water into the base.

Roast the joint for 35 mins per 450g, turning down the oven to 190°C/170°C fan oven/gas mark 5 after 25 mins. Check the water every now and then – you may need to add a few glassfuls if it evaporates. When cooked, remove the crackling, slice the pork and serve with crackling and juices from the pan.

gamberi con funghi selvatici
prawns with wild mushrooms

This easy dish has wonderfully clean flavours and it's really quick to knock up. I stick to the absorption method for cooking rice, as it works perfectly every time, with every grain distinct and separate.

Prep time: 8 mins
Cooking time: 20 mins

SERVES 4

INGREDIENTS

300g long-grain rice
salt and freshly ground black pepper
1–2 tbsp olive oil
3 shallots, peeled and finely chopped
1 garlic clove, peeled and crushed
splash of white wine
200g wild mushrooms, sliced
400g large raw prawns
1–2 tbsp freshly chopped parsley

Weigh the rice, then put it into a jug so you can see the volume, and tip it into a pan. The quantity of boiling water you need is double the volume of rice – for this recipe, that means 650ml, which you add to the pan with a pinch of salt. Cover, bring to the boil, then turn the heat right down to low and leave it alone while it continues to cook, following the timing on the pack.

Heat the oil in a pan and fry the shallots until golden. Add the garlic and cook for 1 min, then add the wine and allow it to bubble up in the pan.

Add the mushrooms with another drizzle of oil and cook until golden. Add the prawns, toss everything together and cook until the prawns turn pink.

Use a fork to fluff up the rice, then divide among four plates. Spoon over the prawn mixture, then sprinkle with the parsley and serve.

pollo alla cacciatora
hunter's chicken

Here's another legendary dish from my father, Vincenzo's, repertoire. The recipe changes from family to family, but the essential ingredients remain the same. It's a selection of chicken joints cooked in an onion and tomato herb sauce. Serve with tagliatelle, polenta or boiled potatoes.

Prep time: 15 mins
Cooking time: 45 mins

SERVES 4–6

INGREDIENTS
1–2 tbsp olive oil
1 onion, peeled and chopped
200g chestnut mushrooms, halved if large
1 garlic clove, peeled and crushed
4 chicken thighs
4 chicken drumsticks
salt and freshly ground black pepper
400g can chopped tomatoes
125ml white wine
a few sprigs of oregano
1 tbsp freshly chopped parsley

Heat the oil in a large sauté pan and fry the onion for about 10 mins until softened. Add the mushrooms and garlic, and cook until golden. Set aside on a plate.

Add another drizzle of oil, if necessary, and brown the chicken pieces in the pan, seasoning as you go. Return the onion mixture to the pan and pour over the tomatoes, wine and 150ml boiling water. Add the oregano. Cover and simmer for 20 mins until the chicken is cooked. Sprinkle with parsley before serving.

Sacla' tip
If you're in a rush, leave out the garlic, onion and tomatoes. Instead, fry the mushrooms in the oil, brown the chicken pieces and then add 400g of Dallaglio by Sacla' Bolognese sauce. Continue with the recipe from this point.

agnello alla piemontese
leg of lamb with rosemary and garlic

Lamb is one of our favourite Sunday lunch joints. It's rich, so a little goes a long way. I always make gravy out of the juices left in the pan, and I add a teaspoon of redcurrant jelly to it at the end of the cooking to balance the flavours.

Prep time: 20 mins
Cooking time: around 2 hours, plus resting

SERVES 4

INGREDIENTS

2.6 kg leg of lamb
2 sprigs of rosemary
2–3 garlic cloves, peeled and sliced
salt
1 tbsp plain flour
100ml dry white wine
300–400ml hot lamb or chicken stock

Preheat the oven to 220°C/200°C fan oven/gas mark 6.

Using a sharp knife, make a few incisions in the lamb. Snip the rosemary sprigs into a few pieces and pair them up with a slice of garlic. Push them into the incisions, then season all over and put in a large roasting tin. Roast for 20 mins.

Turn down the oven to 190°C/170°C fan oven/gas mark 5 and roast the joint for a further 20 mins per 450g.

Take the lamb out of the oven, transfer it to a plate, cover with foil and leave to rest in a warm place.

Drain off and discard all but about 1 tbsp fat from the roasting tin. Put the tin on the hob over a medium heat and add the flour. Stir until bubbling and mixed in with the fat and juices.

Pour in the wine and allow the mixture to bubble up, stirring all the time. Add the hot stock and bring to the boil. Simmer for about 10 mins until thickened and syrupy.

Taste for seasoning, then pour the juices into a gravy jug and serve with the lamb.

costata alla fiorentina
florentine beef

This dish is celebrated all over Tuscany, not just in Florence. Its secret is its simplicity: when you eat it in a restaurant over there, you get it straight from an open-fire grill. It should be slightly charred on the outside and served either rare or medium rare. You can achieve a similar result at home with a good cast-iron griddle pan. All you need with it is a handful of rocket and some potatoes lightly roasted in olive oil.

Prep time: 5 mins
Cooking time: 20 mins

SERVES 4

INGREDIENTS
2 T-bone steaks
2–3 sprigs of rosemary, chopped
a little olive oil
salt and freshly ground black pepper
1 lemon, cut into wedges

Put the steaks in a shallow container with the rosemary, and drizzle with olive oil. Set aside to marinate for 30 mins at room temperature.

Heat a griddle pan to the point where droplets of water falling on it sizzle and evaporate instantly. Season the steaks and fry, one at a time, for about 5 mins on one side and 3–4 mins on the other. Set aside to rest for 10 mins.

Use a meat knife to carefully slice the meat away from the bone, trim any fat, and slice each piece on the diagonal. Serve with the lemon wedges and an additional seasoning of salt.

Sacla' tip
Spoon 4 tbsp Sacla' Classic Pesto over the steak just before you serve it.

bollito misto alla Dallaglio
italian rustic stew

This is my pared-down version of a Piedmontese classic winter dish. If you wanted to cook the traditional recipe, you'd be using ox tongue, veal and beef, which makes enough to feed the entire England rugby team. I've simplified it to chicken and sausage. The sauce that goes with it is a must, as are some plain boiled vegetables alongside, such as potatoes, carrots, baby turnips and onions.

Prep time: 15 mins
Cooking time: 1 hour 15 mins

SERVES 4

INGREDIENTS

1 medium onion, peeled
2 celery sticks
2 carrots, peeled
1 whole chicken
salt and freshly ground black pepper
2 sausages

For the salsa verde

½ garlic clove, peeled
1 tbsp capers
2 anchovies in oil
20g flat-leaf parsley
2 sprigs of basil leaves
1 tbsp white wine vinegar
4–6 tbsp olive oil
salt and freshly ground black pepper

Chop the vegetables into rough chunks and put in a pan. Add the chicken and cover with cold water. Season, cover and bring to the boil. When it has reached a heavy boil, skim away any scum and reduce the heat to a simmer. Half cover the pan at this stage. Cook for 1 hour, then add the sausages and continue to cook for 15 mins.

While the meat is cooking, put all the ingredients for the salsa verde in a mini blender and whiz until smooth. Season well.

Lift the chicken, sausages and vegetables out of the broth, put them on a large platter and keep warm. Bring the liquid up to the boil and simmer until reduced by about a quarter.

Carve the chicken – it'll just fall off the bone – and divide among four plates with some sausage and vegetables. Ladle over some of the broth and serve with the salsa verde sauce.

spigola con pomodori e patate
sea bass roasted with potatoes, tomatoes and olives

This is one of those dishes that you find in many restaurants along the coast of Liguria – the region famous for pesto. It looks impressive and always earns me major brownie points when I serve it up. But, like so much of my cooking, it's actually very simple to knock up. If you have a pan to which everything sticks, then line the bottom with a sheet of baking parchment before you start.

Prep time: 15 mins
Cooking time: 1 hour

SERVES 4

INGREDIENTS
800g potatoes, peeled and sliced
1 large onion, peeled and finely sliced
3 tbsp olive oil
300ml hot fish stock
salt and freshly ground black pepper
2 large sea bass or bream
4 plum tomatoes, halved
a handful of black olives
2 tbsp capers
sprigs of fresh basil

Preheat the oven to 200°C/180°C fan oven/gas mark 6.

Put the potatoes and onion in a large roasting tin. Drizzle with 2 tbsp of the oil and pour over the hot stock. Season well. Roast in the oven for 40 mins.

Slash the fish two or three times on each side, then place on top of the potatoes. Season again. Add the tomatoes, drizzle over the remaining oil and roast for a further 20 mins. Add the olives and capers for the last 5 mins of cooking. The dish is ready when the fish is opaque.

Take out of the oven, sprinkle with the basil and serve immediately.

Try this wine with it...
Ciavolich, Pecorino (Abruzzo)
White

cotechino con lenticchie
sausage with lentils

This is traditionally eaten on New Year's Eve in Italy. It's a great way to feed a crowd because you can make the lentils a couple of days ahead and put them in the fridge, then reheat with a splash of water. Enzo and I love it with good quality pork bangers, but if you can get hold of cotechino sausages from an Italian deli you'll be making the authentic dish.

Prep time: 10 mins
Cooking time: around 30 mins

SERVES 4

INGREDIENTS

1 tbsp olive oil
1 onion, peeled and finely chopped
2 celery sticks, finely chopped
1 carrot, peeled and finely chopped
1 garlic clove, peeled and crushed
200g green or brown lentils
1 bay leaf
650ml hot vegetable stock
1 tomato, chopped
1 tsp balsamic vinegar
8 sausages
2 tbsp freshly chopped parsley

Heat the oil in a large sauté pan and fry the onion, celery and carrot until softened and starting to turn golden. Add the garlic and cook for 1 min.

Add the lentils and bay leaf and stir everything together, then add the hot stock and chopped tomato, and cover and bring to a gentle simmer. Cook for about 20 mins until tender. Stir in the balsamic vinegar.

Fry the sausages in a separate pan. When cooked, serve with the lentils and sprinkle over the parsley.

sacla' tip

For a spicy kick, stir 2 tbsp Dallaglio by Sacla' Diavola pasta sauce into the lentils 5 mins before the end of cooking time.

'Vincenzo, at 28, with his father, Nero (my grandfather), outside the Duomo di Torino in 1962'

stinco di agnello ai funghi
braised lamb shanks with button mushrooms and shallots

Lamb shanks need long, slow cooking, but the result is certainly worth it. They become unbelievably tender and, with this recipe, end up bathed in a fabulously rich sauce.

Prep time: 5 mins
Cooking time: around 2 hours

SERVES 4

INGREDIENTS
1 tbsp olive oil
8 shallots, peeled
1 garlic clove, peeled and crushed
250g button mushrooms
4 lamb shanks
300ml hot chicken or lamb stock
100ml white wine
a sprig of rosemary
salt and freshly ground black pepper
boiled potatoes and steamed
 vegetables, to serve

Heat the oil in a flameproof casserole and fry the shallots for 5–10 mins until starting to turn golden. Add the garlic and cook for 1 min. Add the button mushrooms and cook for 5–10 mins until starting to turn golden, too. Lift out and set aside.

Brown the lamb in the pan. Add the shallot mixture to the lamb, together with the hot stock, wine and rosemary. Season well.

Cover, bring to the boil, then turn the heat down to a simmer and cook for 1–1½ hours, until tender.

Serve with boiled potatoes and steamed veg.

Try this wine with it...
Midolini, Rosacroce Uvaggio Rosso (Friuli)
Red

'Slow cooking means that the meat is so tender it just falls off the bone'

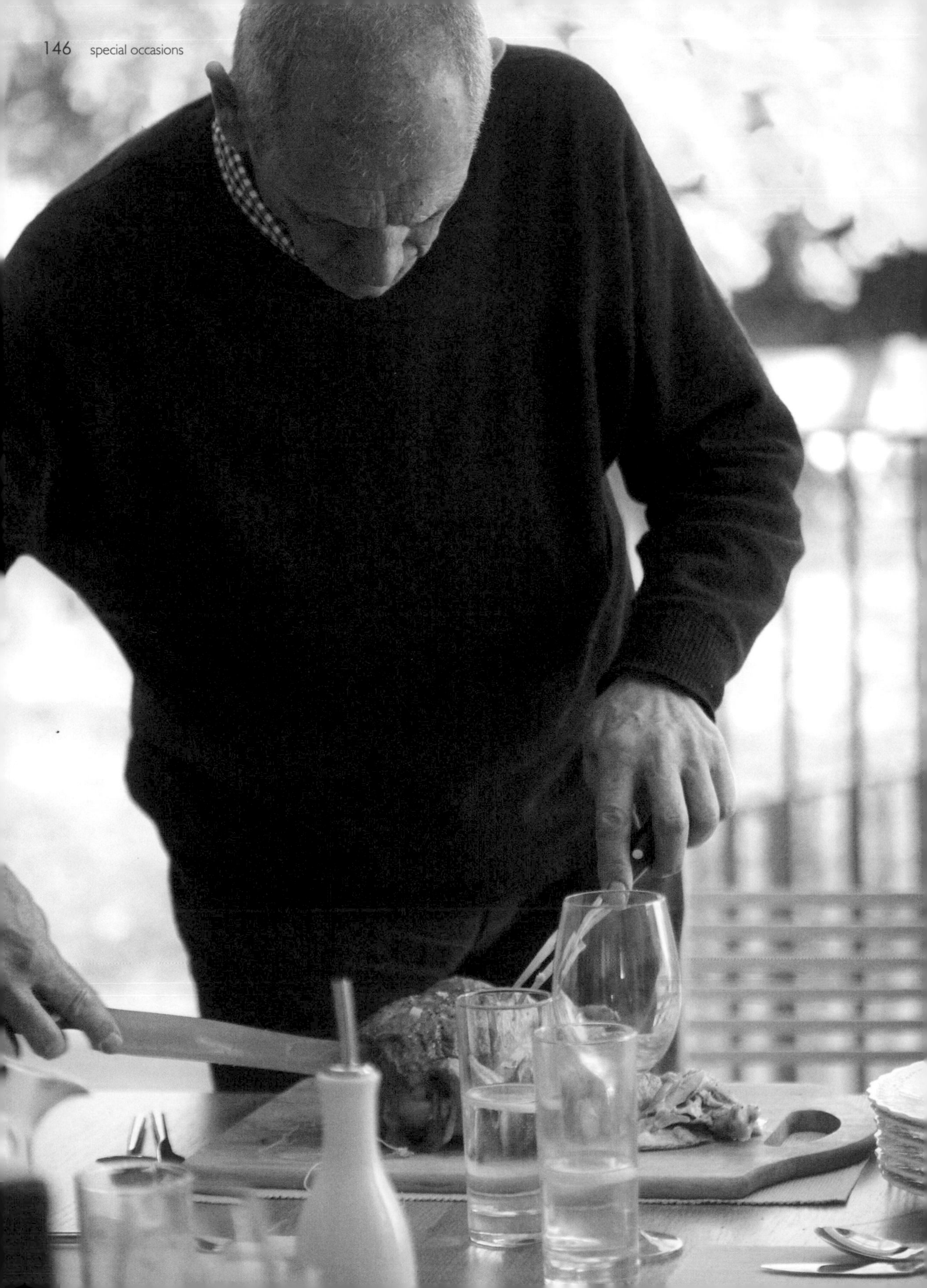

pollo arrosto alla Dallaglio
roast chicken Dallaglio-style

This is roast chicken the Dallaglio way – the difference between this recipe and any other are the ingredients that go into the seasoning. You need sprigs of rosemary and a few garlic cloves, which are stuffed inside the cavity. I mash these into the gravy at the end for added flavour.

Prep time: 5 mins
Cooking time: around 1 hour 20 mins

SERVES 4 with leftovers

INGREDIENTS
1 whole chicken
salt and freshly ground black pepper
2–3 sprigs of rosemary
2–4 garlic cloves (depending on how
    garlicky you like it), unpeeled
1 tbsp plain flour
200ml dry white wine
400ml hot chicken stock

Preheat the oven to 190°C/170°C fan oven/gas mark 5. Season the chicken cavity and stuff the rosemary and garlic in the cavity.

Put in a roasting tin and season all over. Pour a glass of water into the tin. Roast for 20 mins per 450g, plus an additional 20 mins. It's ready when you stick a skewer into the thigh and the juices run clear. If they're pink, continue to cook, checking every 5 mins.

Take the chicken out of the oven and use a spoon to scoop out the garlic cloves. Put on a warm platter and cover with foil. Set aside to rest. Resting the chicken is important, as it gives the juices a chance to run through the meat, maximising its tenderness by the time you carve it.

Drain and discard all but about 1 tbsp fat from the tin. Stir in the flour and place the tin on a hob over a medium heat. Cook for 1–2 mins until golden and bubbling.

Add the wine, stirring all the while, then pour in the hot stock. Squeeze the soft purée from the garlic cloves into the tin. Mash it into the liquid, stirring it in well. Bring to the boil and simmer until syrupy and thickened. Carve the chicken and serve with the gravy.

lasagne all'emiliana
emilia romagna-style lasagne

I can cook this dish with my eyes shut. It originates in the Emilia Romagna region of northern Italy, where my father was born, and has been handed down through generations of Dallaglios. You need nothing more than a mixed green salad tossed in a simple dressing to go with it.

Prep time: 30 mins
Cooking time: around 1 hour 50 mins

SERVES 4–6

INGREDIENTS

500g lean beef mince
1 onion, peeled and finely chopped
1 carrot, peeled and finely chopped
1 celery stick, finely chopped
400g can chopped tomatoes
1 tbsp tomato purée
300ml hot beef stock
100ml red wine
2 bay leaves
salt and freshly ground black pepper
25g butter
1 tbsp plain flour
400ml skimmed milk
nutmeg, to season
6 dried lasagne sheets
50g freshly grated Parmesan cheese

In a large pan, brown the mince in batches. Use a wooden spoon to press it down and break it up into bits as it starts to colour. Transfer the mince to a bowl. Add the onion, carrot and celery to the pan, and cook for 15 mins until softened and starting to turn golden.

Put the mince back into the pan and add the chopped tomatoes, tomato purée, hot stock, wine and bay leaves. Season well. Cover and bring to the boil, then remove the lid and simmer for 45 mins until the sauce has reduced and thickened.

Meanwhile, melt the butter in a small pan. Stir in the flour and cook for 1 min. Add the milk slowly, stirring all the time to make a sauce. Cook for 1–2 mins until slightly thickened. Season with salt, pepper and nutmeg.

Preheat the oven to 200°C/180°C fan oven/gas mark 6. Put a third of the meat sauce in the bottom of a 1.2-litre ovenproof dish. Top with two lasagne sheets, a third of the white sauce and a third of the cheese.

Repeat the process until all the lasagne sheets and ingredients have been used. Cook in the oven for 30–40 mins until bubbling and golden and heated through.

sacla' tip

If you're short of time, use a jar of Dallaglio by Sacla' Napoletana pasta sauce, plus the same jarful of water again, added to the pan of mince at the end of Step 1, and stir in. Bring to a simmer and cook for 10 mins, then stir in 1 tbsp each freshly chopped parsley and basil. Complete the recipe as above.

pollo arrosto con porcini
chicken stew with porcini mushrooms

In Italy, the traditional name for this recipe is *coniglio arrosto con porcini*, and it calls for rabbit legs (*coniglio* means rabbit). I've used chicken here to broaden the recipe's appeal, but if you want to be traditional, order one jointed rabbit from your local butcher and use all of it. Whichever you use, serve it with polenta or mashed potatoes.

Prep time: 15 mins
Cooking time: 1 hour 5 mins

SERVES 4

INGREDIENTS

20g dried porcini
4 chicken drumsticks and
    4 chicken thighs, skinned
8 rashers streaky bacon
1 tbsp plain flour
salt and freshly ground black pepper
2 tbsp olive oil
4 large shallots, peeled and quartered
1 sprig of rosemary
2 sprigs of thyme
200ml dry white wine

Preheat the oven to 200°C/180°C fan oven/gas mark 6. Put the porcini in a bowl and cover with 150ml boiling water. Set aside.

Wrap the streaky bacon around the chicken drumsticks and thighs, and secure with a cocktail stick. Toss in the flour, then season well.

Heat the oil in a pan and fry the chicken pieces until golden all over. Drain the porcini, reserving the liquid, and add the porcini to the pan with the shallots and herbs. Continue to cook until everything starts to brown.

Season well, pour in the wine and mushroom liquid (strain this through a clean cloth first), then cover with a lid and cook in the oven for 30 mins. After this time, remove the lid and cook for a further 15 mins.

Try this wine with it...
Baiocchi, Sagrantino di Montefalco (Umbria)
Red

merluzzo alla veneziana
venetian salt cod

Start this recipe the day before, because salt cod requires soaking overnight. I've simplified the classic *baccalà alla veneto*, which involves cooking the salt cod with onions and oil until soft and tender. Instead, this recipe involves frying the fish in a little flour and serving it with a drizzle of pesto at the end. The combination of salty cod with creamy, buttery polenta is out of this world. Ask your local fishmonger to get hold of it for you.

Prep time: 15 mins, plus overnight soaking
Cooking time: 30 mins

SERVES 4

INGREDIENTS
500g piece of salt cod
1 tsp salt
300g polenta
1 tbsp olive oil
1 tbsp plain flour
50g salted butter
4 tbsp Sacla' Classic Basil Pesto
½ lemon, cut into 4 wedges

Soak the salt cod overnight in a bowl of cold water. The next day, drain, rinse under cold running water, then cut into four equal pieces.

Put 3 litres of cold water in a pan and bring to the boil. Add the salt and polenta and stir furiously, making sure the polenta doesn't contain any lumps. Reduce the heat and simmer, stirring every now and then, for about 30 mins, making sure the polenta doesn't stick to the pan.

About 15 mins before the end of cooking time, heat the oil in a pan until hot. Toss the salt cod in the flour, then fry it in the pan for about 10 mins, turning halfway through, until golden on each side.

Stir the butter into the polenta and divide among four plates. Top with a piece of fish and drizzle 1 tbsp of pesto over each piece of fish. Serve with a wedge of lemon.

cannelloni con ricotta e funghi
cannelloni with ricotta and mushrooms

Cannelloni tubes look fiddly, but they're actually easy to fill – even for rugby players with hands the size of dinner plates! Use a small teaspoon or a spoon handle to push the filling into each tube. When cooked, cannelloni are firmer than pasta you boil in water – that's because they are baked in the sauce, instead of absorbing loads of water.

Prep time: 20 mins
Cooking time: 35–40 mins

SERVES 4

INGREDIENTS

1 tbsp olive oil
2–3 shallots, peeled and finely chopped
1 garlic clove, peeled and crushed
250g mushrooms, finely chopped
1 tbsp chopped thyme
250g ricotta
salt and freshly ground black pepper
300g jar Dallaglio by Sacla'
   Bolognese sauce
12 cannelloni tubes
2 slices white bread, whizzed into
   breadcrumbs
25g freshly grated Parmesan cheese
green salad, to serve

Heat the oil in a pan and fry the shallots and garlic until softened. Add the mushrooms and thyme and cook until all the juices have been absorbed. Tip into a bowl, cool a little, then mix in the ricotta. Season well.

Preheat the oven to 200°C/180°C fan oven/gas mark 6.

Spoon the Bolognese sauce into a bowl and add 150ml cold water to the jar. Shake to dislodge the bits inside the jar and pour into the sauce. Stir well. Spoon a little into the base of a 1.2-litre ovenproof dish.

Stuff the ricotta mixture equally into the cannelloni tubes. Place in the dish on top of the sauce. Cover with the rest of the tomato sauce. Scatter over the breadcrumbs and cheese, and season. Cook in the oven for 30 mins until golden and bubbling.

Serve with a green salad.

Try this wine with it...
Alpha Zeta, Valpolicella Ripasso (Veneto)
Red

tortelloni di zucca
butternut squash-stuffed pasta

This is the celebratory supper that my grandmother used to give us on Christmas Eve. It makes the most of ingredients that are seasonal in December, with a few store cupboard stalwarts thrown in for good measure. It's a feast that's light, as you don't want to peak too soon when you've got a day of serious eating ahead.

Prep time: 45 mins, plus 20 mins resting time
Cooking time: 40 mins

SERVES 4

INGREDIENTS
600g butternut squash
salt and freshly ground black pepper
200g 00 pasta flour, plus extra for dusting
2 large eggs
4 amaretti biscuits
15g freshly grated Parmesan cheese
nutmeg, for grating
1 egg yolk, beaten
melted butter

'In our house, the men do the Christmas cooking'

Preheat the oven to 200°C/180°C fan oven/gas mark 6.

There's no need to peel the squash, just cut it in half lengthways, scoop out and discard the seeds, then put it in a roasting tin, flat-sides up. Season and roast for 20–30 mins until tender.

Make the pasta dough. Sift the flour onto a clean board or work surface and crack the eggs into the centre. Use a fork or clean fingers to mix together the egg and slowly draw in the flour.

Continue to work the flour in until you make a dough. Knead briefly until soft and sticky. Cover with clingfilm and leave to rest for 20 mins.

Scoop the squash flesh into a bowl, discarding the skin. Crush the amaretti biscuits and stir into the squash with the Parmesan. Season with salt, freshly ground black pepper and a little nutmeg.

Divide the dough into quarters and roll out each piece into long rectangles using a pasta machine. Dust and clean the work surface, and place the first rectangle of pasta on it. Cut it in half widthways to make two smaller rectangles.

Roughly divide the filling into four portions. Then divide each portion into five and place each spoonful, evenly spaced, onto the sheet of pasta. Brush egg yolk around each blob of filling, then gently lay the other piece of pasta on top. Press the pasta down over the filling, making sure there's no air inside. Cut around the blobs to separate each piece. Repeat with the remaining dough to make 20 pieces in total.

Bring a large pan of water to the boil and cook the pasta in batches for a few minutes. Divide among four plates, drizzle with melted butter and grind a little black pepper on top.

Try this wine with it...
Cortegiara, Bardolino (Veneto)
Red

petto di tacchino ripieno
stuffed turkey breast

Christmas Day is a practice run of small courses, building up to the main event: stuffed turkey breast. The important thing here is to season the turkey at each stage; that way you'll get a flavoursome joint. I also use a good, coarse bread – even a seeded brown loaf – to give the stuffing texture. My father, who has been involved with food all his life, makes it an annual habit to remind my kids (and me) to wash hands before and after handling raw poultry to avoid spreading germs around the kitchen.

Prep time: 30 mins
Cooking time: around 2½ hours

SERVES 8

INGREDIENTS

25g butter
1 small onion, peeled and finely chopped
50g sultanas
40g pine nuts
80g country bread, chopped
2 sausages, skinned
leaves pulled from a few sprigs of thyme
a few sprigs of sage, chopped
1 medium egg
a splash of white wine
salt and freshly ground black pepper
100g pancetta
around 3 kg turkey breast
2 tbsp plain flour
200ml dry white wine
600ml hot turkey or chicken stock
1 tbsp redcurrant jelly

Preheat the oven to 200°C/180°C fan oven/gas mark 6.

Melt the butter in a pan and sauté the onion for about 10 mins until softening and turning golden. Stir in the sultanas and pine nuts and cook for 1 min. Tip into a bowl and set aside to cool. Once cooled, add the bread pieces, sausages, herbs and egg, and mix together. Moisten with a splash of wine and season well. Mix again.

Lay the pancetta on a chopping board, each slice slightly overlapping the other. Place the turkey breast on top, skin-side down. Use a knife to cut into the turkey flesh along the length of it to create a pocket. Season well and push the stuffing evenly into the pocket, then replace the turkey flap to cover.

Cut five or six lengths of string long enough to go round the turkey. Slip them under and along the width of the turkey, and tie tightly to keep everything together. Flip over, place on a plate and weigh. Calculate the cooking time and roast for 15 mins per 450g, plus 15 mins. Put in the roasting tin and pour a glass of water into the base, cover with foil and roast in the oven. Keep topping up the water every 20 mins or so. Remove the foil 20 mins before the end for the pancetta to brown nicely.

To test if it's cooked all the way through, insert a skewer into the thickest part of the joint and check the juices run clear. If not, continue to cook, checking every 5 mins.

Put on a warm plate, cover with foil and set aside. Drain and discard all but 1 tbsp fat from the roasting tin. Add the flour to the tin and place over a medium heat. Stir it into the juices and cook for 1–2 mins until it's bubbling and looks paste-like. Pour in the wine, stirring all the time, then gradually stir in the hot stock. Add the redcurrant jelly. Bring to a simmer for about 5–10 mins until thickened and syrupy. Taste to check the seasoning. Pour the gravy into a warm jug and serve with the turkey.

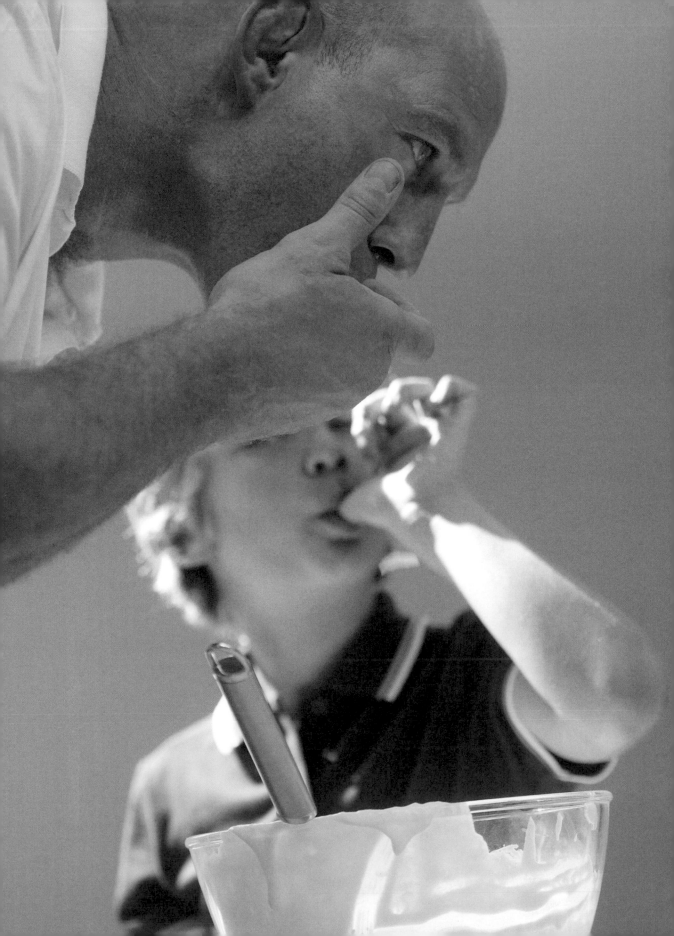

dolci
sensazionali

sensational desserts

5

It's hard to imagine a brute like me making delicate fillings for pastry confections, but a good pud is a work of art that delights the senses. Increasingly, though, the kids bag making that part of the meal.

cioccolata calda
hot chocolate

Here's a twist on two highly addictive items: hot chocolate and chocolate puddings. It needs to be served as soon as you spoon it into the bowls, so it's a make-between-courses pud – but as long as you have everything prepared, it will only take a few minutes.

Prep time: 15 mins
Cooking time: 5 mins

SERVES 4

INGREDIENTS

100ml double cream
2 tsp icing sugar
250g dark chocolate, broken into pieces
4 tbsp rice flour
200ml milk
2–3 tbsp caster sugar
1 tbsp amaretto liqueur
2 amaretti biscuits, crushed

Whisk the double cream with the icing sugar until soft and mousse-like. Chill.

Put the chocolate pieces in a pan and pour over 100ml cold water. Melt the chocolate over a medium heat.

Add the rice flour and use a wooden spoon to mix all the ingredients together, stirring all the time, until thickened – it won't take long.

Slowly add the milk, caster sugar and liqueur, and whisk constantly until smooth and thick. Spoon into four 150ml ramekins, top with a dollop of chilled whisked cream and a sprinkling of amaretti biscuits, and serve immediately.

affogato al caffè
ice cream with espresso

You could be forgiven for thinking that with a list of just two ingredients, who needs a recipe? *Affogato al caffè* translates as 'drowned with coffee', but it's the way the 'drowning' is balanced that makes or breaks this dessert. Too much coffee and the ice cream melts into a mess; too little and you'll just have a revoltingly sweet dessert. This balance is just right.

Prep time: 5 mins

SERVES 4

INGREDIENTS
a tub of vanilla ice cream
200ml hot espresso coffee

Scoop the vanilla ice cream into balls and put one or two scoops each into four small bowls that have been chilled in the freezer first.

Pour 50ml of coffee into each of four espresso cups and let everyone drown their own ice cream!

panna cotta ai frutti di bosco
traditional Italian cream pudding

This recipe is very rich, so even I reckon that a little goes a long way. I use less gelatine than in most recipes, because I like a softer texture when it's set. Serve with a tumble of berries in summer, or poached plums in winter.

Preparation and cooking time:
30 mins, plus overnight chilling

SERVES 4

INGREDIENTS
3g gelatine leaves
200ml double cream
200ml full-fat milk
1 vanilla pod, split lengthways
75g golden caster sugar
summer berries, such as raspberries,
 blueberries and strawberries, to serve

Soak the gelatine in a small bowl of cold water.

Put the double cream, milk and vanilla pod in a pan and bring just to the boil. Turn off the heat and leave to infuse for 30 mins.

Add the sugar and stir to dissolve. Lift the gelatine out of the water and add it to the cream. Stir to melt, then strain the mixture through a sieve and into a jug.

Pour among four 110ml ramekins, or dariole moulds if you have them. Cover and chill overnight.

Dip each mould briefly into a bowl of boiling water, then carefully run a knife around the inside to dislodge the contents. Turn onto plates and scatter over the berries. Enjoy.

torta al limone
lemon tart

You can cheat and buy a ready-made lemon tart, but there's nothing to beat a homemade one – especially this one. Besides, it's Alice's all-time favourite, so my share price rises sharply every time I produce it.

Prep time: 30 mins, plus 40 mins chilling
Cooking time: 1 hour 20 mins

SERVES 10–12

INGREDIENTS

1 quantity sweet pastry (see page 187), chilled for 20 mins
4 medium eggs
175g golden caster sugar
175ml double cream
zest and juice of 3 lemons
icing sugar, to dust

Preheat the oven to 200°C/180°C fan oven/gas mark 6.

Roll out the pastry and use it to line a deep 23cm fluted round tart tin (see my tips on the Apple and frangipane tart recipe on page 187). Cover with a piece of baking parchment and chill for 20 mins.

Fill the covered pastry with baking beans (you can use rice or uncooked dried beans, too) and bake in the oven for 15–20 mins until dry to the touch. Remove the beans and the baking parchment, and continue to cook for 5–10 mins until completely dry. Turn down the oven to 150°C/130°C fan oven/gas mark 2.

In a bowl, mix together the eggs, sugar and double cream. Stir in the lemon zest and juice – you'll notice the mixture thicken: that's the acid combining with the cream. Pour into the pastry case and bake for 50 mins until just set. Leave to cool in the tin.

Remove the tart from the tin, dust with icing sugar, then slice and serve.

Try this wine with it...
Pieropan, 'Le Colombare' Recioto di Soave (Veneto)
Sweet white

zabaglione
frothy italian custard

This classic boozy dessert is said to have originated in Piedmont. The heat holds the egg yolks, sugar and wine together, so as soon as it's whisked, don't delay getting it to the table, as it needs to be eaten straightaway.

Prep time: 20 mins

SERVES 4

INGREDIENTS
3 medium egg yolks
40g golden caster sugar
125ml Marsala wine
Italian biscuits or langue de chat, to serve

Put the egg yolks, sugar and wine together in a large glass bowl. Rest over a pan of simmering water, making very sure that the base doesn't touch the water.

Whisk the ingredients together until the mixture forms soft peaks and the texture is mousse-like.

Spoon into four individual glasses and serve with the biscuits.

'The egginess almost persuades me that zabaglione is mainly about protein...'

torta con nocciole e cioccolato
chocolate and hazelnut cake

This cake involves chopped, toasted hazelnuts in a rich chocolate sponge. Eat it any way you like – either as an afternoon pick-me-up, or as a pud with a dollop of mascarpone. Chop the nuts in a food processor, if you like, but don't over-whiz them or they'll turn greasy and the cake will be heavy.

Prep time: 20 mins
Cooking time: 40–50 mins

SERVES 10

INGREDIENTS

125g unsalted butter, chopped,
    plus extra for greasing
100g blanched hazelnuts
150g dark chocolate (minimum 70%
    cocoa solids), broken into pieces
4 medium eggs
150g golden caster sugar
50g plain flour
1 tsp baking powder
mascarpone and cocoa powder, to serve

Grease and line a 20cm loose-bottomed round cake tin with baking parchment. Preheat the oven to 180°C/160°C fan oven/ gas mark 4.

Toast the hazelnuts in a dry frying pan until golden. You'll know when they're ready, as there'll be an amazing aroma of roasted nuts driving your taste buds crazy. Finely chop them.

Put the chocolate in a bowl and melt over a pan of simmering water, making sure the base doesn't touch the water. Don't touch the chocolate until it has all melted, otherwise it can 'seize' and thicken.

Add the chopped butter to the bowl and allow it to melt in slowly, then stir. Remove the bowl from the heat and set aside to cool.

Whisk the eggs and sugar in a bowl for about 5 mins until soft and mousse-like in texture. Fold the chocolate into the mixture, then the chopped nuts, flour and baking powder.

Spoon the mixture into the tin and bake for 40–50 mins, until the top of the cake feels firm when pressed. Remove from the tin onto a plate. Cool a little, then slice, and serve with a dollop of mascarpone and a dusting of cocoa powder.

'My daughter, Josie, is a total chocaholic —
she press-ganged her brother and sister
into helping to make their mum a birthday
cake. Pretty good effort'

zuccotto toscano
frozen tuscan dessert

This dessert originated in Tuscany and is one of those brilliant recipes that needs very little expertise, but makes you look terrific. Buy whole, candied peel and chop it yourself. You'll find it at the supermarket in boxes of lime, lemon and orange. Choose whichever flavour floats your boat.

Prep time: 20 mins, plus overnight freezing

SERVES 6–8

INGREDIENTS

240g plain sponge cake
juice of 1 large orange
2 tbsp brandy
150ml double cream
1 tbsp icing sugar, plus extra to dust
25g dark chocolate, grated
60g glacé cherries, chopped
40g candied peel, finely chopped

Line an 800ml pudding basin with clingfilm to make it easier to turn out the contents at the end.

Slice the cake and use it to line the sides and base of the pudding basin, making sure every bit of the bowl is covered. Keep a little bit of cake left over to cover the filling.

In a bowl, mix together the orange juice and brandy, and spoon all over the sponge.

In a separate bowl, beat the double cream and icing sugar together until thick enough to just hold its shape. Fold in the chocolate, cherries and candied peel, and spoon the mixture into the basin and level. Cover with the remaining slices of sponge cake, then cover with clingfilm. Freeze for at least 8 hours.

Remove the pudding from the freezer and turn out onto a plate. Take off the clingfilm and dust with icing sugar before serving.

'A Dallaglio joint venture — making pancakes in the Farinet Hotel kitchen in Verbier, 2008'

biscotti all'arancia e nocciole
hazelnut and orange biscuits

These biscuits are traditionally enjoyed at the end of the meal with a glass of Vin Santo – Italian dessert wine. You can buy them in any deli, but making them is a cinch and they keep for ages in an airtight container. I like the hazelnuts with skins on, as they give more flavour.

Prep time: 10 mins
Cooking time: 1 hour, plus 10 mins
   cooling

MAKES ABOUT 32 BISCOTTI

INGREDIENTS
2 medium eggs
225g granulated sugar
80g hazelnuts
50g unsalted butter, melted
1 tsp baking powder
zest of 1 orange
325–350g plain flour

Preheat the oven to 190°C/170°C fan oven/gas mark 5.

Whisk the eggs and sugar together in a large bowl or in the bowl of a mixer until pale, thick and mousse-like – this will take about 5 mins. Fold in the hazelnuts, melted butter, baking powder, orange zest and enough flour to make a smooth, slightly sticky dough. Bring together with your hands and knead roughly on a board.

Split the dough in half and shape it into two long, flat rectangles about 23 x 7cm each. Place them on a baking sheet lined with baking parchment and bake for 20 mins.

Take out of the oven and allow to cool on the baking sheet for 10 mins. Line another baking sheet with baking parchment.

Reduce the oven temperature to 150°C/130°C fan oven/gas mark 2. Slice each long piece of baked dough on the diagonal into 1.5cm slices. Lay the slices flat on a baking sheet and bake for a further 40 mins, turning over every 10 mins until cooked through and pale golden. Leave to cool on the baking sheets, then pack into airtight containers and store for up to a month.

macedonia di frutta
fruit salad with cinnamon and spice

This sweetly spicy syrup turns a fruit salad into an occasion, and makes it a favourite in the Dallaglio household in winter.

Prep time: 15 mins
Cooking time: 5 mins

SERVES 4

INGREDIENTS
50g golden caster sugar
juice of ½ orange
1 cinnamon stick
1 kg fruit, such as apples, oranges, grapes, mango, kiwi fruit and pineapple

Put the sugar in a pan with the orange juice and cinnamon stick. Add 100ml cold water. Bring to the boil and simmer for about 3–4 mins until the sugar has dissolved and the liquid is syrupy. Allow to cool.

Prepare the fruit: slice the apples and segment the oranges and put them in a large bowl. Cut the grapes in half, if you like, and chop the mango into chunks. Peel and chop the kiwi fruit and pineapple.

Pour the syrup over the fruit and leave to macerate for a couple of hours before serving.

semifreddo alla vaniglia
speedy vanilla ice cream

No need for an ice-cream machine to make this lighter-than-air confection
– just whisk all the ingredients together. We flavour it simply with vanilla and
serve it with a selection of sliced fruit.

Prep time: 20 mins, plus chilling
and freezing

SERVES 8

INGREDIENTS
1 vanilla pod
600ml double cream
4 medium eggs, separated
125g golden caster sugar

Slit the vanilla pod in half lengthways, then run the rounded end of
a table knife along the length of each half to scrape out the seeds.
Transfer to a small bowl.

In a separate large bowl, whip the double cream until thick and
moussey. Fold in the vanilla seeds, then chill in the fridge.

Whisk the egg whites in a clean, grease-free bowl until stiff peaks
form. Add 1 large spoonful of the sugar and whisk it in. Set aside.

In a separate bowl, whisk the egg yolks with the remaining sugar
until doubled in size. Next, fold the chilled cream into the egg yolk
and sugar mixture until they are combined.

Fold a large spoonful of the beaten egg whites into the mixture
until mixed in, then fold in the remainder.

Spoon the mixture into a sealable container and freeze for at
least 8 hours.

pere cotte nel vino rosso
pears cooked in red wine

This dessert couldn't be easier and, best of all, you can make it up to three or four days in advance. Make sure you turn the pears every 10 minutes or so, so that all sides get poached evenly in the wine.

Prep time: 15 mins
Cooking time: 45 mins

SERVES 4

INGREDIENTS
4 pears
300ml red wine
75g golden caster sugar
pared zest of ½ orange
1 cinnamon stick, broken

Peel the pears, leaving the stalks intact, and use a sharp knife to remove the calyx at the base.

Put the red wine in a medium pan, big enough for the pears to fit snugly in the base, with the sugar, orange zest and cinnamon stick. Add 100ml cold water. Heat gently to dissolve the sugar.

Add the pears, cover with a piece of scrunched up greaseproof paper and cover with a lid. Covering the pears with greaseproof paper will create steam within the pan, which will poach the pears beautifully.

Bring to the boil, then reduce the heat to low and cook for 45 mins, tossing the pears halfway through. Lift out of the pan and put each on a dessert plate. The liquid will have reduced to a fantastic syrup – divide this among the pears and serve immediately.

torta di polenta con arancia
orange and polenta cake

No baked pudding captures the spirit of Italy more than the ones that include polenta and are flavoured with oranges. Polenta is yellow cornmeal, and it can be coarsely or finely ground. Here, you need the fine type so that the texture isn't gritty. This pud is a big hit at home.

Prep time: 20 mins
Cooking time: 45 mins

SERVES 10

INGREDIENTS

175g unsalted butter, plus extra
   for greasing
3 oranges
200g unrefined caster sugar
3 medium eggs, beaten
200g self-raising flour
50g fine polenta

Grease and line the base of a 22cm round cake tin with baking parchment.

Slice two of the oranges thinly (you'll need enough slices to cover the base of the tin, so one and a half oranges may be enough). Put the slices in a large pan with 150ml water. Bring to the boil and simmer for a few minutes to poach.

Lift out the orange slices and place them in the base of the tin. Add 2 tbsp of the sugar to the liquid in the pan and bring to the boil. Simmer until the liquid is syrupy and reduced by half. Pour the syrup into the prepared tin over the orange slices.

Preheat the oven to 190°C/170°C fan oven/gas mark 5.

Zest the remaining orange and squeeze to extract the juice. Put the butter and remaining sugar in a bowl and cream together until light, pale and fluffy. Gradually add the beaten eggs, then fold in the flour with the orange zest, juice and polenta. Mix everything together.

Spoon the mixture into the tin and level. Bake for 35 mins or until a skewer inserted into the centre comes out clean. Cool in the tin for 10 mins, then tip the cake out onto a plate, cut into slices and serve with vanilla ice cream (see page 175).

'There's nothing incongruous about a former rugby player baking!'

tiramisù
'pick me up' pud

'Pick me up' is the literal translation of *tiramisù* and you can see why, given the caffeine in the espresso and cocoa. Add to these two ingredients sweet mascarpone mousse, sponge biscuits and Marsala wine, and it's pretty wicked, even as desserts go.

Prep time: 15 mins, plus chilling

SERVES 6

INGREDIENTS

3 large eggs, separated
75g icing sugar
300g mascarpone
100ml espresso or strong black coffee,
    cooled
2 tbsp Marsala wine or rum
18–20 Savoiardi biscuits (sponge fingers)
cocoa powder or dark chocolate
    (minimum 70% cocoa solids)

In a bowl, whisk the egg yolks, icing sugar and mascarpone together until combined.

In a separate clean, grease-free bowl, whisk the egg whites until stiff peaks form. Fold one spoonful of the egg whites into the mascarpone mixture to loosen, then gently fold in the remainder.

Put the coffee and Marsala in a shallow bowl. Dip half the Savoiardi biscuits into the coffee liquid and line a 1.2 litre serving dish with the soaked biscuits. Spoon over half the mascarpone mousse.

Repeat with the remaining biscuits, dipping them in the coffee, and finish with a layer of mascarpone mousse. Dust with cocoa powder or finely grate a little dark chocolate over the top.

Chill for at least a couple of hours to set, then remove from the fridge 30 mins before serving.

torta di formaggio con limone
lemon cheesecake

Although biscuit-based cheesecakes are the norm here, the sponge-based, European style is the one I prefer. If life's too short to make it from scratch, buy a ready-made sponge flan case and use the base of the tin as a template to cut out a circle. Alice is crazy about lemony puddings, so ours tend to get eaten as soon as they come out of the oven, but they're best if they chill overnight, as the flavours come together and the texture becomes firm and creamy.

Prep time: 20 mins
Cooking time: 1 hour, plus overnight chilling

SERVES 12

INGREDIENTS
For the base
10g unsalted butter, melted,
    plus extra for greasing
1 medium egg, at room temperature
50g golden caster sugar
zest of ½ lemon
50g self-raising flour

For the topping
600g full-fat cream cheese
100g golden caster sugar
3 large eggs, separated
zest of 2 lemons
½ tsp vanilla extract
juice of 1 lemon

Grease and line a 20cm round spring-form cake tin with baking parchment. Preheat the oven to 160°C/140°C fan oven/gas mark 3.

Make the sponge base. Whisk the egg and sugar together in a bowl until soft and frothy and the mixture leaves a ribbon-like trail.

Add the lemon zest, flour and melted butter, and gently fold all the ingredients together. Bake in the oven for 15 mins until the cake is golden and 'squeaks' slightly when pressed on top. Leave to cool.

To make the topping, beat together the cream cheese, sugar, egg yolks, lemon zest, vanilla extract and lemon juice.

In a clean, grease-free bowl whisk the egg whites until stiff peaks form. Fold 1 tbsp into the cream cheese mixture, then add the remaining egg whites and gently fold everything together.

Pour into the prepared tin, on top of the sponge, and bake for around 45 mins. Cool in the tin, then chill overnight before serving. Remove from the fridge 30–60 mins before serving to allow the cheesecake to reach room temperature.

crostata di more e prugne
plum and blackberry crumble with amaretti

This is a fruity concoction that uses the best late-summer fruit and is an ideal sweet ending for Sunday lunch. Once your oven is free after cooking the roast, put the crumble in and it'll be ready when you've finished eating the main course. To make it slightly healthier, you can swap half the flour for wholemeal flour. Serve with ice cream, a drizzle of double cream or custard.

Prep time: 15 mins
Cooking time: 40 mins

SERVES 6

INGREDIENTS
For the fruit
9 plums, halved and stoned
225g blackberries
2 tbsp light muscovado sugar
1 tsp ground cinnamon
½ tsp ground ginger
juice of ½ orange

For the topping
175g plain flour
125g unsalted butter, chilled and cubed
50g amaretti biscuits, crushed
25g flaked almonds
25g light muscovado sugar

Preheat the oven to 200°C/180°C fan oven/gas mark 6.

Put the plums and blackberries in a large bowl. Add the sugar, spices and orange juice, and toss everything together. Spoon into a 27 x 20cm shallow ovenproof dish.

Sift the flour into a large bowl. Add the butter and rub in roughly – there should still be a few clumps of butter. Stir in the crushed amaretti biscuits, flaked almonds and sugar.

Spoon the topping evenly over the fruit and bake in the oven for 40 mins.

sorbetto all'arancia
orange sorbet

This is a zingy and refreshing, palate-cleansing sorbet. If you leave out the egg white and rough it up with a fork, you get the other classic Italian ice, granita.

Prep time: 20 mins, plus freezing

SERVES 4

INGREDIENTS
6 large oranges
150g golden caster sugar
1 medium egg white

Zest two of the oranges and set the zest aside.

Use a sharp knife to cut away the peel and pith from all the oranges, revealing the orange segments. Cut in between each section of orange skin to remove the segments.

Put the segments in a blender and whiz to make juice. Pour into a jug – you should have 600ml liquid.

Put the juice in a pan with the sugar and heat gently to dissolve the sugar. Pour into a sealable freezer-proof container, and cool. Freeze for a couple of hours until firm and crystallised, but not frozen solid.

Scoop out the frozen juice and put in a blender again with the egg white. Whiz to combine. Pour back into the container and freeze until solid.

'Orange sorbet is summer on a plate – an echo of my long school holidays spent in Italy'

crostata di marzapane alle mele
apple and frangipane tart with pine nuts

You can buy sweet pastry, but my kids like to make it. You have to blind-bake the pastry first (bake it first on its own, without the filling), otherwise its base won't cook and will end up soggy. The finished dessert is stunning, but it's very rich, so serve it in thin slices with a spoonful of thick cream.

Prep time: 30 mins, plus 40 mins chilling
Cooking time: 1 hour 20 mins

SERVES 10–12

INGREDIENTS
For the sweet pastry
200g plain flour, plus extra for rolling out
100g chilled unsalted butter, diced
1 medium egg yolk

For the filling
350g cooking apples, peeled, cored and chopped
2 tsp golden caster sugar
1 tsp plain flour
a good pinch of ground cinnamon
150g unsalted butter, softened
150g golden caster sugar
1 medium egg
1 tbsp plain flour
150g ground almonds
50g pine nuts

Start by making the pastry. Put the flour in a food processor and add the butter. Whiz until it feels like sand. In a small bowl, mix the egg yolk with 1 tbsp water and pour in. Whiz again until the mixture forms slightly bigger clumps. It should still look crumbly.

Tip into a bowl and bring together with your hands, kneading lightly to make a soft dough. Shape into a disk, wrap in clingfilm and chill for 20 mins.

Roll out the pastry on a lightly floured board or clean work surface. Use it to line a deep, 23cm fluted flan tin. Cover with a piece of baking parchment and chill for 20 mins. Preheat the oven to 180°C/160°C fan oven/gas mark 4.

Fill the parchment-lined tin with baking beans (you can use rice or uncooked dried beans, too) and bake for 15–20 mins until dry to the touch. Remove the beans and baking parchment, and continue to cook for 5–10 mins until completely dry.

Toss the apples, sugar, tsp flour and cinnamon together in a bowl, and scatter over the base of the pastry.

Beat the butter and sugar together in a bowl until soft and creamy, then beat in the egg. Fold in the tbsp flour and ground almonds.

Spread over the apples to cover – a palette knife is ideal for pushing the mixture down. Scatter with the pine nuts and bake in the oven at the same temperature for 50 mins. If the pine nuts look like they're going to burn, cover with a sheet of foil.

Cool the tart in the tin until either warm or completely cold, and serve with thick cream.

Try this wine with it...
Deltetto, Arneis Passito 'Bric Liun' (Piedmont)
Sweet white

index

Buon appetito!

Sun-ripened tomatoes, fragrant sweet basil, pungent onions, celery, garlic, herbs and olive oil – these form the basis of Italian cooking. Simplicity is the key: the sun concentrates flavours, so top-quality, fresh ingredients harvested at the peak of their perfection don't need much help in delivering a big flavour punch. This is what defines the Sacla' philosophy.

Dallaglio collection

This is the range that Dad and I produced with Sacla'. We took a long time in our own kitchen and then at the development kitchens at Sacla' in Italy, and we're very proud of what we've achieved. We hope you enjoy cooking with them as much as we enjoyed creating them.

DALLAGLIO BY SACLA' DIAVOLA

'Diavola' means 'little devil', and this certainly qualifies. Fiery red chillies and garlic combine with vine-ripened tomatoes in an Italian classic.

DALLAGLIO BY SACLA' TRICOLORE

Soft and creamy mozzarella, sweet vine-ripened tomatoes and fragrant basil – a true Italian sauce that's perfect for pasta.

DALLAGLIO BY SACLA' BOLOGNESE

Onions, carrots and celery mingle with tomatoes and herbs, infused with a generous glug of local Barbera red wine.

DALLAGLIO BY SACLA' NAPOLETANA

Fresh-tasting, chopped tomatoes and basil combined with onion, carrot and celery – wonderful stirred through pasta, or as a base for something more complicated.

DALLAGLIO BY SACLA' ITALIAN SLOW-BAKED TOMATOES MARINATED WITH CHILLI

Italian plum tomatoes peeled, oven-baked and marinated in oil and piquant chilli. Fabulous on pizza, sandwiches or in any tomato-rich sauce.

DALLAGLIO BY SACLA' ITALIAN SLOW-BAKED TOMATOES MARINATED WITH GARLIC

Rich and succulent tomatoes, slowly baked, then marinated in oil and tangy garlic and capers, rich in vitamins and antioxidants.

Sacla' collection

Italian food without basil, Sacla' pesto's key ingredient, is unthinkable. Herbs are central to the nation's cooking, but among them, basil is king. There are over 20 varieties, but sweet basil is the one most commonly used in the Italian kitchen: with its pungency and distinctive aroma, released the moment you brush its leaves, for me it's synonymous with everything that is glorious about Italian food. Sacla' produce many sauces, but these are the ones I can't do without in our kitchen...

SACLA' CLASSIC BASIL PESTO

An aroma of freshly picked basil, the rich release of crushed pine kernels and a hit of newly grated Grana Padano cheese.

SACLA' SUN-DRIED TOMATO PESTO

Fragrant basil, sun-dried tomatoes, Grana Padano cheese and, as with all great pesto sauces, crushed pine kernels. Mellow, but intense.

SACLA' ORGANIC TOMATO PESTO

A vivid blend of organically nurtured, aromatic basil, sun-dried tomatoes, extra virgin olive oil and crushed pine kernels.

SACLA' ARTICHOKE ANTIPASTO

Tender and irresistible quarters of Italian globe artichokes, traditionally prepared with flat-leaf parsley in clear, golden oil.

SACLA' TOMATO & OLIVE BIG BOLD ITALIAN SAUCE

Italian tomatoes and olives left to become plump and ripe in the glorious Mediterranean sunshine, in a robust, chunky stir-through sauce.

Acknowledgements

This book could not have happened without the help and support of so many people. Enormous thanks are due to Hilary Ivory and Nigel Wright, who as editor and art director, made our words and ideas come alive; to home economist Emma Marsden who, assisted by Charlotte Dunne, had the job of testing all our recipes and making sure that our measurements and cooking times were accurate; to Ruth Jenkinson, for capturing the most beautiful pictures of my family in action in the kitchen, around the table, and in the garden; to Steve Baxter for his absolutely stunning food photography; and to my assistant, Rachel Bayes, for keeping my life organised and on track.

I'm also grateful to the Ercole family at Sacla' in Italy, who make our sauces and, of course, to Clare Blampied, the Managing Director of Sacla' UK, and her team, who work tirelessly to promote our Dallaglio by Sacla' sauce range. Thanks, too, to my publishers, Simon & Schuster UK and, in particular, editorial director, Francine Lawrence, who not only believed that a rugby player can also cook real food, but helped me produce the book I wanted.

Of course, the people who deserve the greatest thanks are my family. My father, Vincenzo, for having the patience, time and energy to educate me from an early age on everything he knew about food and wine. And for what stability there is in my life, I must thank my beautiful wife, Alice, and our three amazing children, Ella, Josie and Enzo.

Finally, I dedicate this book to the memory of my sister, Francesca, whose last conversation with me was at the table sharing a family meal on the night she died; and also to my late mother, Eileen, who supported me every step of the way and who gave me the unshakable belief that it wasn't just okay to shoot for the moon, it was essential.

Photos not taken specifically for the book are by Sim Canetty-Clarke (wedding picture of Alice and me), Getty Images (me playing rugby), and from the Dallaglio and Ercole family albums.